Backward into Light

B44/03

Backward into Light

The Passion and Resurrection of
Jesus according to Matthew and Mark

J. L. HOULDEN

SCM PRESS LTD

British Library Cataloguing in Publication Data

Houlden, J. L.
Backward into light: the passion and
resurrection of Jesus according to
Matthew and Mark.
1. Jesus Christ———Passion 2. Jesus Christ
———Resurrection 3. Bible. N. T. Matthew———
Commentaries 4. Bible. N. T. Mark———
Commentaries
I. Title
232.9′6   BT400

ISBN 0–334–00067–X

First published 1987
by SCM Press Ltd
26–30 Tottenham Road, London N1

Typeset at The Spartan Press Ltd,
Lymington, Hants
and Printed in Great Britain by
Richard Clay Ltd, Bungay, Suffolk

For Barry

CONTENTS

Foreword   ix

1 Hearing the Gospels   1

2 Matthew among the Gospels   13

3 From Gift to Assault   20

4 From Resignation to Requital   41

5 From Intimation to Demonstration   55

6 Villains and Realists   66

   Epilogue: Post-critical Spirituality   74

   Notes   79

   Index of Biblical References   83

FOREWORD

This book belongs to a well-known genre. The genre arises from the custom in a number of theological colleges of inviting someone to give special lectures in Holy Week. This book consists of Holy Week lectures delivered in 1986 at Salisbury and Wells Theological College, then fed and watered until they reached their present stage of maturity. I am grateful to Reggie Askew, the Principal of the College, for his initial invitation, for the welcome given to me by the College as a whole, and so for the opportunity to make this book.

The lectures formed but one ingredient in the observance of Holy Week. There was also – and chiefly – the liturgy of the week, in a setting of much silence; as well as 'happenings' which presented relevant passages from the Gospels. Within this whole, the aim of the lectures was, first, to see what happened at a crucial stage in Christian reflection on Jesus' death and resurrection, towards the end of the first century: its first writing down in a continuous narrative, and then the re-working of that story by a subsequent writer. The further aim was to see how such a process may speak to us after all these years.

Though the book is not heavily exegetical, part of its context is that of modern New Testament studies, with their wide range of methods. Among these, some are especially appropriate to the present task, as chapters 1 and 2 will show. But there is also here a concern to go beyond New Testament studies as, in present practice, a self-contained discipline. From one point of view, there is perfect validity in taking those studies as a distinct sphere of enquiry; but from another, there must always be interest in what the New Testament may betoken and how it is now to be 'heard'. If integrity is to be preserved, that requires some kind of marriage between such truth as emerges from New Testament studies, with their historical and literary preoccupations, and the life and beliefs of the modern reader whose interests are not purely historical or literary. The principles on which such a marriage may be achieved are not particularly clear, not an agreed matter, and there is room for exploration. When one engages in that exploration, one invites a general theological audience to give attention.

In expressing this interest, this book follows on from my *Connections*, 1986. In the text, I often refer to the present work as an 'exercise'. It is based on ideas discussed in the earlier book, for like many writers, I really only have one tune to play. I now apply those ideas to these crucial passages in the Gospels of Mark and Matthew which tell of Jesus' death and resurrection. It is an attempt to enable them still to speak – and enable us to face the consequences.

I am grateful to those who, sometimes in the distant past, have helped to form my mind on these matters, especially Christopher Evans, John Fenton, Michael Ramsey, and W. H. Vanstone.[1] I am also grateful to Alan Race for quickening my wits in the period of writing and for helping Edwin Muir to give me my title, to Simon Duckworth for encouragement, and to Jill Fuller, Stephen Barton and Nicholas Bradbury for help at the time of the delivery of the lectures.

Passages from the gospels are printed in the Revised Standard Version.

I

Hearing the Gospels

Once, not so long ago, the study of Christian theology took place within an extensive and orderly programme of enquiry. Most of those who undertook it were aspiring professionals – would-be clergy or teachers. They could, for the most part, be depended upon to have been grounded in a certain body of knowledge and skills. They knew what it was to learn a language other than their own; they had acquired a sense of literary and historical framework. Upon these foundations, the conventions of theological education could build, in the study of the Bible, the history of the church and the formation of its doctrine. Here was a coherent and delimited educational process. At each stage, it was possible to know with some assurance what attainments to assume and what further goals to seek.

These things are no longer so. At every point, diversity has prevailed. Those who undertake courses of theological study are of many kinds: not just aspiring professionals but those whom publishers designate hopefully 'interested laypeople'. And the professionals themselves, whether would-be clergy or teachers, look towards a much more diversified field for their operations, culturally and ethnically. Many intellectual perspectives press for their attention, and they enter upon their studies with all kinds of different educational equipment and experience, giving little for those who teach them to take uniformly for granted. In such a context, theology itself, in its various branches, has widened its horizons, extending the range of its methods and questions, and drawing upon academic disciplines to which it was formerly unrelated.

It is then no wonder that universally helpful landmarks are harder to come by. It is not likely that the same programme of theological study will be effective for both a thirty-year old biochemist and a twenty-five year old accountant, both perhaps training for the church's ministry; and neither will take easily to the literary, historical and conceptual skills which have become inseparable from the modern study of Christian theology and are indeed, at a deeper level, built into its very structure. For Christianity has no identity if it does not attend to certain historical episodes relating to Jesus and the story of the church, to the ancient writings in the Bible which alone give access to the most crucial and influential of those episodes, and to the heritage of ideas in which Christians habitually clothe their faith.

No one should underestimate the difficulties created by this situation for one who seeks to engage in theological writing with the hope of being not just informative but, more, useful and intelligible to people beyond the tiny handful of the experts. There is informative theological writing in abundance: telling the history of ancient Israel, the nature of the biblical writings, or giving an account of some period in Christian history or some aspect of Christian belief. But there is, necessarily, an appetite for what is also useful, that is, theological reflection which at some point makes contact with experience, with what is otherwise felt to be significant and valid, and which is somehow fertile, leading the reader outwards, towards the total structure of his thought and the pattern of his life. Not only useful but also intelligible; that is, making contact with what is already known as true, integrating with it fruitfully and not just lying alongside it as so much extra stock in one's storehouse of information.

Any theological writing which has any chance of passing these tests must be sensitive to multiple dangers (of being use*less* and *un*intelligible) and so, in regard to the factors they bear upon, sophisticated; but at the same time, it must be demonstrably and constantly related to fundamental and elementary matters, for it cannot make many assumptions about skills and needs possessed in common by a body of readers. It must in any case run the risk of being found appealing by those who happen to share something of the writer's own formation and baffling by those who do not.

In the quest for usefulness and intelligibility, there is the further danger that those alert to these problems will lose contact with Christian identity. That is, in their concern to 'speak to' the interests and thinking habits of modern secularized people (for be we never so Christian in the heart's allegiance, all of us are pervasively people of our time and place), their relationship with the Christian tradition becomes merely formal and skin deep. Even if the will is there, it seems increasingly hard to use the Christian past, including the Gospels which tell of our beginnings, in a way that both does justice to modern study of them and goes beyond the most generalized edification or else abstract dogmatic statement hard to interpret in 'real life' terms. Modern historical study of the Gospels, by its very success and efficiency, has more and more placed them firmly in their first-century setting and thus accentuated their status as products of that age rather than as living scriptures addressed to people of any time whatsoever. Can justice be done both to what is now understood as true about the Gospels as historical documents and to the Christian's wish to 'lay hold' of them in theological reflection?

The purpose of this book is to conduct a limited exercise in the use of the Gospels. It takes a sample of Gospel material, the story of Jesus' suffering, death and resurrection, as told in the Gospel of Matthew alongside that of Mark. It 'worries' it from a number of quite limited angles, in order to see what can now be received.

The innocent reader will think such an exercise both unexceptionable and straightforward. Why does the writer approach his task so lengthily and circumspectly? Why does he not, after the briefest of explanatory prefaces, simply get down to it? For surely, there can be nothing deeply problematic or complex about a study of the passion and resurrection narrative in the Gospel of Matthew or

Mark that aspires to be both academically open-eyed and
conceptually interesting. Yet, our simplest actions have a background which, in our haste or our simplicity, we generally ignore
but which, brought to our notice, can enrich our understanding.
The first section of this chapter sketched something of what may be
regarded as the middle background of our exercise. There are also
remoter and nearer backgrounds which are worth surveying.

The discussion of the middle background noted certain tensions
to which this book is a response and which it sets out at least not to
ignore. The remoter background is full of deeper conflicts and
severer tensions which (to state a conviction) are much too often
neglected and by-passed in both theological and ecclesiastical
circles. In relation to the latter, they lie, rarely attended to, at the
root of many current debates, whether about negotiations for the
union of churches, or reforms like the ordination of women, or the
standing of traditional beliefs such as the virginal conception or
physical resurrection of Jesus.

This is not the place to discuss that remoter background in
detail, still less the particular issues just referred to. It was the
subject of the opening chapters of an earlier book.[1] All the same, it
will be helpful to recall its leading features. The spirit in which this
is done is not coldly factual. While being as realistic as possible, we
aim to turn what may be felt as a predicament into an opportunity.
Victims of our past, we are also creators of our future, with choices
open to us. Here then are some leading features of the remoter
background, viewed in that realistic and yet hopeful light.

1. The religious impulse presses us towards a unified response
of the whole person, indeed, as far as possible, of the whole
community, even the human race, to God. It seeks to bring all
aspects of ourselves into harmony before him. In so far as that
includes our minds, it comes into conflict with the essentially
analytical procedures of most modern intellectual effort. Those
procedures seek to distinguish one realm of enquiry from another,
to intensify its special skills and perspectives; and moreover, to
conduct its investigation in a spirit of detachment from ideo-

logical and universalizing tendencies. Analytical enquiry will even seek to banish the encroachment of those tendencies by ever more refined awareness of them. There is then a profound gulf between the religious impulse and the procedures of theological enquiry.[2]

2. As these procedures have for long – and irreversibly[3] – dominated theological studies, along with all others, there has been a shift in the very meaning of 'theology' as a subject of human thought.[4] Once, over the greater part of the Christian period, it signified the quest for God by the human mind, using the data of nature and of revelation. Its heart lay in what we now call spirituality; but it moved out easily and without awareness of plainly marked frontiers into what now goes under the heading of doctrine and ethics, and it involved the use, in ways now rarely found,[5] of scripture and Christian writers of the past, seen as authorities. Its unified state is what chiefly strikes the modern observer looking back, all the more so as he then turns to view what theology now signifies: a plethora of distinct intellectual disciplines,[6] each with its own conventions and agenda, each constantly developing and refining itself in the context of wider academic life, and each taking little trouble to knit up with its companion studies, which also go under the name of 'theology', or showing much feeling for engagement in a common grand enterprise. And yet the individual and the church, with lives to lead and as consumers of 'theology', must face, simply cannot renounce, the task of achieving a unified theology, but have only these unpropitious modern tools to help them; unless they still take up the tools of the past, taking them from the well-stocked Christian store (or museum), as week-end enthusiasts dress up as Cavaliers and Roundheads to fight again the battles of the English Civil War.

There is no difficulty in tracing the origins and development of these two major sources of difficulty. Reformation and Enlightenment suffice as labels for their earlier stages. Now none, resist or regret as they may, can escape their influence. Even those who hold most fast to a theological outlook which by-passes or reckons to antedate them are not only, inevitably, made to look like survivals, but are even compelled to play by their rules. Thus, so powerful now is sensitivity to the fact of historical change and to anachronism that sheer traditionalism stands out all the more clearly in its datedness, its pedigree easily exposed, and its failure to absorb the insights and often the sheer facts of the present made plain. So powerful and obvious now is the pluralism of opinions and beliefs that even the strongest adherent of the role of authority in religion acts subjectively in selecting the creed to which he submits. In that sense, European culture has made 'protestants' of even the most ultramontane Catholics. One may accept or reject the force of theological reasons for welcoming the present situation in theology, both in its tensions with the religious impulse and its fragmentation; one may (that is) take it as a predicament or as an opportunity. What one cannot do is to hope for a fruitful hearing in 'the real world', pretending it to be other than it is. Suppose, however, that one accepts that force. Suppose that the present, with all its apparently unfavourable features for faith, is the God-given framework within which (rather than despite which) one must now be Christian and serve God. Then, just as we cannot turn away from social and economic realities as providing the setting in which Christian decisions must be made, so neither can we turn away from changed realities of the mental scene, the present sense of what which 'cannot but be true'. There is undoubtedly a choice. It is possible to live, sadly, in the light of the maxim that 'he who marries the spirit of the age will soon find himself a widow', preserving thereby a rather negative style of virtue; or it is possible to recognize that when Christianity has wooed the spirit of the age, it has, with infinite polygamy, made one vigorous and fruitful marriage after another, however hard some of its partners have been to catch and however unlikely they may initially have looked as potential spouses. To resist courtship at all may lead to unfortunate consequences: one may be captured against one's will, so contributing little to the subsequent union. Christianity has sometimes known that fate. Or else, outwardly protesting resistance, it has been seduced in many aspects of its life. Freely entered marriage must be more promising and more admirable than either outcome.

Suppose then that we try for that goal. Then speedily we move forward to the middle background with which we began. We seek to think (or write) theology that is authentically Christian, bearing the clear marks of Christian identity, and yet regrets nothing of truth that has been given to us, even today, *this* 'day which the Lord has made'. So we return to our exercise, which concerns that brief span of composed narrative, the story of Jesus' passion and resurrection in the Gospel of Matthew, and, as we shall see, even that from a limited point of view. How quickly, yet how necessarily, have we moved from the widest features of Western culture to a narrow instance of human activity. Yet we must see to it that we have lost nothing on the way. The broadest aspects all have their bearing on the smallest instance. The deepest characteristics of our cultural past and present all find a presence within our reading of those final chapters of the Gospel. For the story is not just the property of Jesus, whose momentous death it tells, or that of the evangelist who recorded it long ago in his own little world of thought and sensibility, but of each of us who read with our own personal (yet also communal) eyes. It is then time to move forward again, now to the nearer background to our exercise.

The Gospels are indispensable for Christian identity. But what use is to be made of them? We can treasure them and honour them – and that may be quite compatible with, in practice, ignoring them or feeling their impact only momentarily, perhaps in the course of an onward flowing liturgy. Or we can tap into the rich and ever accumulating store of scholarly study of the Gospels. Despite its age – two centuries at least – its results still remain largely in a segregated world, unfamiliar to many who might be expected to use them; like a game whose rules are felt to be too complex for it to be played by any but specialists. Yet the essence of the matter is of the utmost accessibility. What does the modern study of the New Testament seek to achieve? Only to hear the writer's voice, to enter his mind, to see the framework of his life – and so to grasp his meaning. It is, surely, a laudable aim. For think of the alternative: to read his words as if they were our own words, meaning what we should have meant if we had written them; or else what we should have liked him to have meant by them. Many human conversations are conducted, many books are read, on that principle, and its practice can scarcely be avoided wholly. But as in social life we count its minimizing a virtue and failure to exercise it a coarse weakness, so in our relationship with an author and with a text – such as, now, the Gospel of Matthew. The task is to *hear* the voice that addresses us, and graciously to permit it to be different from our own.

Put differently, the task is to interrogate the author in order to elicit meaning. Interrogation may involve a multiplicity of questions. Notoriously, as any pollster knows, the questions help to determine the answers gained. So it is not surprising that in questioning a text, which is not necessarily formed so as to respond to what is asked of it and is but a partial precipitation of the total setting which can alone explain it, the possibility of divergence, contradiction and fruitless quest is considerable. Illumination may be fitful or even illusory. The interrogation of an ancient text is not a pastime for those determined to reach assured results. Nevertheless, anyone who would not wish to cease attending to the text and who sees the dangers of making it the mere mouthpiece of his own assumptions and beliefs, has no alternative but to persist. He is likely, if he is a cautious spirit, to be seeing more light than he is prepared to admit.

The range of questions is not difficult to recognize. It is a roll-call of the successive techniques which New Testament scholarship has used in the course of its development.[7] Given the making of all copies by hand until the late fifteenth century, what was the evangelist's precise wording? What earlier writings had he before him as sources for his work? Did he have other, oral sources, and, if so, how were they formed and whence did they derive? Does his work betray consistency of literary style, language, and thought? If so, what can we learn of the writer's preoccupations and beliefs?

may we even learn something of his social setting and that of the Christian group to which he belonged? What, then, were its similarities to and differences from other Christian, Jewish and pagan groups of the time? Then two final and quite disparate questions: What can we know (from the Gospel itself and any other relevant sources) of the true career of Jesus himself? For all history writing distorts as well as discloses. And what total story was the writer setting out to tell?

There is a tendency for present Gospel study to push in two divergent directions. One is acutely conscious of history, the other lays such awareness aside in attentiveness to the text itself. The former is concerned to identify, so far as the evidence allows, the setting of a Gospel and its author, within the Christianity of the later first century. There it began; there, initially, it belongs, however people may later receive and use it, making it serve their purposes and moulding its sense with the pressure of their piety or their dogma. So there let us attend to it, in its first setting, allowing it to 'be', to rest – or rather to live, in the busy setting of a Christian group, living cheek-by-jowl, perhaps, with Jews and Greeks, having specific problems to contend with and decisions to make, under the vivid impulse of Jesus, God's Son and Israel's crucified yet triumphant Messiah. For that 'attending', it is necessary to summon the greatest possible degree of historical sensitivity.

The other direction of study forswears, austerely, these concerns. Let us rather follow the flow and logic of the text, attend to its story, grasp its structure and hence its message. Certainly we must know what these words then signified, establish their sense; but the text is our quarry, the focus of our enquiry, or, if we will, the inner momentum of the writer's mind – but then, the two are one, for we know not a thing about him apart from *this text*.

There has been much discussion about the difference between these two tendencies of interpretation, and some weight of opinion, especially from the literary side, in favour of their incompatibility:[8] the 'world' of the text is to be accepted as self-contained and not extending beyond itself into the external events and human affairs of the Gospels' first-century setting, still less the actual life of Jesus.

But such a rigid separation is not self-evidently helpful and the decision to keep them distinct, though justifiable conceptually, seems stultifying if the object is the widest possible understanding of the text in its setting. In the exercise that follows, both will contribute in their place. For its aim, we return to our starting-point: we wish to hear the writer's voice and to share his thoughts, not obtruding ourselves more than we must. Then, having performed our task of sympathy, we indeed become ourselves again, in our time and place, and we see how the text has changed us and has formed us in our attentiveness to God.[9] In the course of that aspect of our task we shall not refrain from assessment of what we have 'heard'. It does not tyrannize over us, but invites our discriminating response. And the exercise of judgment at that point does not vitiate the objective element in the previous enquiry, the attempt to 'hear'.

From an existential point of view, that of the modern reader living in his own time, there would be little profit in hearing the evangelist's voice if his message proved to be trivial. The Gospels may indeed be worth listening to as ancient texts and, in that historical perspective, their study amply justified. And, in the Christian context, their venerability as holy texts, taking their place in liturgy or in the stock of holy objects, may be unimpaired. But the question of their present inherent usefulness, their power to 'speak' effectively, remains to be answered. Their chance of echoing significantly, old though they are, in modern Christian minds depends on their capacity to present the story they tell in such a way that it can affect, even determine, our deepest attitudes and choices.

Among those areas of choice, we instance three: first, the question of our freedom before God; second, the place of morality in our relationship with him; and third, the character of our acceptance of religious truth. In all these areas, we are presented with alternative courses of action and alternative policies in the Christian tradition itself. To take the three examples in turn: there is the question of the part legitimately played in our adherence to God by any kind of pressure exercised upon us or felt by us, whether in terms of miracle or impressive experience: is faith to be the naked response of love to God in himself or something evoked or backed by alleged outworks of his presence? Then: there is the question of the part played in our relationship with God by moral sanctions and scales of justice, as in the life of society, held over us and inevitably colouring our motives and actions: is goodness to be the naked response of love to God for his own sake or something stimulated by the hope of reward and the fear of punishment, and by law interposed between ourselves and God? Then: there is the question of the part played in our understanding of God by compelling evidence or argument: is the truth concerning him open to our grasp, so that we can rest satisfied with what we have understood, or is it for ever elusive, beckoning us onward? The three instances merge into one, that of our adulthood in relation to God. Adulthood not in the sense of assertiveness or mere possession of some selfish right to self-determination, but in the sense of the inner integrity and freedom of the self in relation to God. It is the quality encapsulated in the Johannine sense of confident upward aspiration, yet solely by God's free gift: 'No longer do I call you slaves . . . but I have called you friends' (John 15.15). And the single resulting question is: how 'serious' is God about the bestowing of this gift? Or else: how 'serious' dare we be in accepting it?

What we ask of the Gospels in these matters is not that they should deliver final verdicts (that would be to make them already take sides on the questions posed above), but that they should illuminate them for us; nor that they should themselves stand beyond assessment by us, but that in our own wrestling with the questions, we should be assisted by those who wrestled before us. We should see that the stories of Jesus' death and resurrection do not leave us without aid.

They can perform this service because they are stories of events in which God (says Christian faith) gives himself precisely in order that such understanding may arise. For it is only through the stories, however they may be further mediated to us, that we can encounter the events, and only through the interpretations of them which we attain, that we can find them salvific, re-making our 'worlds', intertwining with our own personal stories in such a way

Backward into Light

that well-being with God is the outcome.

The choices of perception which we have instanced will come before us again as we conduct our exercise. We shall find them confronting us already in the first written narrations of Jesus' death and resurrection, as Mark and Matthew conveyed those events into story form for the sake of the faith of those around them.

2

Matthew Among the Gospels

Our exercise focusses chiefly on the Gospel of Matthew, though always in context and especially in relation to the Gospel of Mark. For the Gospel of Matthew does not stand alone. Particular and specific though its own composition and setting were, towards the end of the first century, it was one element in a rich and varied process of remembering the life and significance of Jesus. Once it had been written, the Gospel soon exercised a wide influence. Speedily, by the early second century, it became well enough known and valued to be quoted by others. And it was not long before it was the most widely used work of authority, above all for Jesus' teaching, given, it was held, by the pen of one of his apostles.[1]

It is interesting to reflect that the reasons for its widespread adoption as an aid or authority may well have borne little relation to the reasons for its composition: so soon may writings move from their original setting and purpose. Thus, it is likely that Matthew's usefulness may be ascribed to its being so rich a store of Jesus' teaching. More than any other of the Gospels, it could be appealed to for his rulings and counsels on a number of important ethical matters. Yet that same feature of the Gospel is likely to owe its origin more to the concern of the writer with the precise relationship between the rules for Christian behaviour and the Jewish Law, a question of pressing urgency in his own background and formation. In Matthew's view, that Law was to be both accepted and yet amplified and transcended in the light of Jesus; and the manner in which that combination of policies was to be accomplished was a matter of the utmost delicacy. That was a need not precisely shared by those who succeeded Matthew and received his book so gratefully as the guide for Christians.

It is also likely that the speed with which this Gospel came to the fore, leaving Mark, in all probability its main source, in the shade, owed much to its bearing the name of Matthew the apostle. As that ascription is almost certainly fictitious, here is another shift away from the origins of the book, whose first readers presumably knew exactly who the author was.[2]

Thus, the Gospel of Matthew soon took its part in forming the future. It also came out of a past. It drew upon the memory and the tradition of Jesus' life. There is no way of demonstrating conclusively the precise forms in which that tradition had been enshrined, especially in its earlier stages. But plainly it came to exist in other written forms in two or three decades on either side of the Gospel of Matthew. Of that fact the other early Gospels are the testimony. Moreover, at least those of Mark and Luke bear close literary relationship to Matthew. The relationship is especially close in the case of Mark, to the extent that almost all of Mark's material has a parallel in the longer work of Matthew.

This relationship, so obvious to modern eyes, seems to have eluded the first person to comment on the Gospel's origins, Papias, who wrote within half a century of their composition: that is a salutary reflection on any tendency to assume that the oldest testimony is the most reliable and true. The relationship was recognized by the fourth century, though not in such a way as to give rise to close analysis of its nature and possible explanation. Not until the late eighteenth century was there either the ethos of historical imagination or the objective interest in the literary phenomena of the Gospels that could make possible well-grounded hypotheses about these matters. Even so, it has not proved possible to demonstrate beyond doubt how the first three Gospels are related to each other, in order of composition and in the use by each of others by way of source.

Several possibilities are still in the field: that Matthew was the first to write, followed by Luke, and then by Mark, the abbreviator; that Mark wrote first, followed by Matthew, and then by Luke, who availed himself of both, though in different ways; that Mark was used independently by both Matthew and Luke, who also had access to a further written (?) source, long since lost. These matters are of interest and importance for gaining a picture of the Gospels themselves, but especially for considering the process by which the tradition concerning Jesus developed, once it reached written form.[3]

But despite the formidable amount of scholarly energy devoted to them, for some important purposes relating to the understanding of the Gospels, these questions of relationship are not of primary importance. While undoubtedly the hypothesis of Mark's priority has long won most adherents, and was for many years virtually a dogma of New Testament criticism, for the purpose of our present exercise it is sufficient to note the *fact* of the differences between the passion story as told in Matthew and in Mark. In what follows I shall in fact write in terms of Matthew's having made alterations to Mark (I believe that to be what occurred), but nothing essential to the purpose of this enquiry will depend upon that assumption of Mark's priority. What will matter is the 'grasping' of Matthew's story – the flow and the force of the narrative. And that will be set off by its contrast with the story as told by Mark,[4] seen by most scholarly opinion as his predecessor in the work. We shall then also take it that, whatever sources he used, each evangelist stood by his story as he arranged and worded it – he did not just write things down mindlessly as they reached him.

What of the passion narrative in itself? There is much to be said for the view that in certain ways it stands apart – either alone or with an account of the resurrection – from the rest of the tradition concerning Jesus. Objectively, as we observe it within the Gospels, in all four cases it forms an integrated piece of writing to a greater degree than any other extensive portion of the narrative of Jesus' life. Though it contains some episodes that are detachable, for the most part the story flows on as a continuous narrative, one thing simply following another and needing to do so if the story is to hang together. Moreover, nowhere else do we have such a concentrated treatment of a brief part of Jesus' life as that which is given to its end.

Though other parts of the story convey a superficial impression of continuous sequence in the progress of his life, that impression is almost certainly illusory and artificial.[5] Closer inspection reveals that most episodes prior to the passion are in fact self-sufficient, only loosely related to the context they have received; and common-sense may confirm that it is much more likely that stories were remembered and told about Jesus independently of each other rather than in a precise and ordered temporal framework.

Moreover, it is not out of place to think of reasons why the story of Jesus' passion should have had this special concentration and integratedness. There is no doubt that this was the part of Jesus' career which first gave rise to belief about him. Christian commitment was to Jesus, but above all to Jesus crucified and raised from the dead. Surely then the story which gave backing and substance to that faith will have been at the heart of Christian memory. Surely too it is likely that this story above all stories about Jesus played a part from earliest days in the liturgical life of the Christian movement – perhaps rehearsed at the anniversary of the events, perhaps much more frequently.[6] There are then strong reasons, some firmer than others, for seeing the story of Jesus' dying and rising as having a special place in the tradition about him which antedated the written Gospels and lay behind them.

All the same, the distinctiveness of the narratives of these events must not be exaggerated. Specially cohesive and concentrated they may be, but they are identifiably part and parcel of the books whose final sections they form. Growing appreciation of the consistency of theological and religious outlook in each of the Gospels, and of the extent to which a single mind has impressed itself on whatever earlier material has been incorporated, has fortified this understanding of them. There are very good reasons for seeing Mark's passion and resurrection story as Marcan, Matthew's as Matthean – and so on. Indeed this consistency and drive of theological purpose was commonly discerned in these stories before it was so readily perceived in other parts of the Gospels.[7]

The approach to Jesus' death through the stories, while it uses the most solid evidence available to us (words on pages), is only one of two major ways of considering these events. Its character will become clearer if we put the two side by side; in any case, the two need to be distinguished and not, as often happens, in the interests of some quest for 'the whole truth' of the matter, unthinkingly merged.

The other approach is through ordinary historical enquiry into the circumstances of the time, beginning with what can be known of the relevant Roman legal institutions and the structure and character of the Jewish leadership in Jerusalem, and moving inwards as closely as the evidence allows towards the particular case of Jesus of Nazareth. The movement is thus one of clarifying the focus on contemporary circumstances. It is then quite distinct in its concern from the more specific but considerably later testimony of the Gospels. Moreover, the approach is free from the intense theological commitment of the Gospel writers, and less subject to the kind of error that arises from the conveying of tradition in circles like the early churches. They were, surely, neither particularly expert in some important aspects of the subject in hand (e.g. legal and governmental technicalities) nor primarily interested in telling the story accurately for mere accuracy's sake. This second approach asks not, What history lies behind the narration of the Gospels?, but, How, at that time and in that setting, might such a one as Jesus have met this end?

In that enquiry, there is an element of objectivity, but also much of hypothesis and of piecing together of relatively meagre evidence. The closer it gets to the case of Jesus and the more detailed the account sought, the greater the degree of shadow and of falling back on intelligent guesswork. Nevertheless, the attempt is far from fruitless and recent reconstructions along these lines are likely to be close to acceptable truth.[8]

The former approach to Jesus' death, by way of narrative, places the element of objectivity in a different place – in the very structure and flow of the stories themselves. Each of the four, while doubtless drawing us towards what 'really happened', initially invites us to share the writer's understanding of it, and so his picture of its meaning. Inescapably, it feeds the reader not with bare knowledge of the course of events but with a view of their significance. Unashamedly (the word reveals the suspicion that shame might be in order!), it steps into the events that gave rise to the story and narrates them in such a way, using interpretative conventions of the time,[9] that the writer's belief about them will be apparent.

The elementary experiment of comparing the four stories quickly reveals that the pictures differ. The modern reader is then tempted either to dismiss them as unreliable or to use ingenuity to reconcile them. The task is impossible and the effort is vain, for it mistakes the nature of the material. What is more, the diversion of energy in that direction prevents the reception of the writer's primary gift – what he wished to communicate as the truth and the meaning of Jesus' death and resurrection.

Now, in this light, there is an immediate difficulty concerning Matthew's account, the chief subject of our exercise. It is, on a sheer line by line viewing, remarkably close to that of Mark. Suppose (it is not essential to the argument but convenient for the presentation) that Matthew used the Gospel of Mark as his chief source – the model which, in his own work, he chose to improve or correct. Then, while in much of the rest of his book, and especially in respect of its wider patterning of material, he modified Mark, and indeed, by his lengthy insertions, entirely altered its structure and balance of contents, when it came to the passion he may be felt to have altered very little. It might seem that here he felt a special reticence or that there was some impropriety in making substantial changes. Was it that the story of these crucial events had already something of the sacredness of liturgy? Or else – it is not impossible – here he had little of his own to communicate, for his dominant interests lay elsewhere. For him, Jesus was primarily the messianic saviour and teacher, God's Son who fulfilled prophecy at every turn and called the heavy laden to accept the gentle yoke of obedience to him.[10] Of course, his death was important, a necessary part of the path he must tread, and the gateway to his triumph which guaranteed his presence with his own; but still, it was not so full of doctrinal meaning that it impelled Matthew to give it a treatment of his own, one notably different from that which he found in Mark, his model and source.

There may be truth in this solution, but it is not the whole of the matter. The special elements in Matthew's narrative are indeed mostly small in extent and, on the surface, not crucial in import. But they are nevertheless his own, and he took trouble to include them. More, in even the smallest actions a writer can reveal a world. Indeed he cannot help revealing his own world. And the more casual (it may seem) his contribution, the more it may be worth attending to. It is no exaggeration to say that to every act we bring our whole genetic, cultural and educational inheritance. How then does Matthew reveal – or betray – himself as he retells the story?

In the next three chapters, we shall discuss three different kinds of passage peculiar to Matthew's story; or, on the commonest view, three kinds of alteration he made to Mark. Each is represented by more than one example, whether from these final chapters of the Gospel or from earlier parts. It will become apparent that each kind of passage represents a facet of Matthew's outlook which is wholly characteristic – and which moreover distinguishes him from Mark. Taken separately and then together, these aspects of the Gospel may then take us further afield in the task of interpreting and using the Gospels.

3

From Gift to Assault

In this first of three central parts of this study, I want to consider two passages from Mark and the parallel to each in Matthew. Before reading the Matthean passage in each case, we should recall that we take a step beyond merely juxtaposing them, though that is enough to make comparison possible. We make the working assumption that Matthew actually had the text of Mark by his side and worked closely with it, line by line. His reworking is, we suppose, wholly deliberate. Comparison then involves a constant testing whether it is a matter of significant intention or merely stylistic preference, of ideas or words. If the former, can we sufficiently penetrate Matthew's mind to identify that intention? Can we at least identify his general attitude?

Was he, for example, saying as he read Mark and then re-wrote his story: 'I know it did not happen so, but rather thus'? Or was it rather: 'I believe that Mark told the truth, but I shall not let that truth stand'? Or else: 'I neither know nor care what happened on that day as Jesus died (or rose), but I shall tell the story so as to impress upon you its momentous meaning'? It puts a salutary brake on our easy assumption that we can just pick up a Gospel, read it, and grasp it, and indeed 'learn' the history behind it, when we face those options, all of them (it seems) possible as ways of accounting for the fact of Matthew's altering of Mark. Certainly any of them would be possible for *us* if we were undertaking such a task.

Yet in all probability none of them represents Matthew's mind, for all involve modern choices and modern sensibility (concerning matters like the ethics of plagiarism and the value of factual accuracy). It is likely that at this first stage in our enquiry, fascinating as it is, we must admit defeat. While, as we shall see, we can attempt to identify the significance of the changes, the frame of mind which brought them about, which expressed its own different 'world' by these means, baffles us. It is a defeat not to suppress but to keep constantly in mind.

Recall that the aim of the exercise is to 'listen' to the Gospel writers, with the detachment that comes from intruding ourselves as little as possible, but still from within faith, as ourselves involved with the story which is related. As we have just seen, both a measure of failure and the prospect of success lie before us.

And when the sixth hour had come, there was darkness over the whole land until the ninth hour.

And at the ninth hour Jesus cried with a loud voice, 'Eloi, Eloi, lama sabachthani?' which means, 'My God, my God, why hast thou forsaken me?'

And some of the bystanders hearing it said, 'Behold, he is calling Elijah.' And one ran and, filling a sponge full of vinegar, put it on a reed and gave it to him to drink, saying, 'Wait, let us see whether Elijah will come to take him down.' And Jesus uttered a loud cry, and breathed his last.

And the curtain of the temple was torn in two, from top to bottom.

Now from the sixth hour there was darkness over all the land until the ninth hour.

And about the ninth hour Jesus cried with a loud voice, 'Eli, Eli, lama sabachthani?' that is, 'My God, my God, why hast thou forsaken me?'

And some of the bystanders hearing it said, 'This man is calling Elijah.' And one of them at once ran and took a sponge, filled it with vinegar, and put it on a reed, and gave it to him to drink.

But the others said, 'Wait, let us see whether Elijah will come to save him.' And Jesus cried again with a loud voice and yielded up his spirit.

And behold, the curtain of the temple was torn in two, from top to bottom; and the

And when the centurion, who stood facing him, saw that he thus breathed his last,

he said   'Truly this man was the Son of God!'
(Mark 15.33–39)

earth shook, and the rocks were split; the tombs also were opened, and many bodies of the saints who had fallen asleep were raised.   and coming out of the tombs after his resurrection they went into the holy city and appeared to many.   When the centurion and those who were with him, keeping watch over Jesus, saw the earthquake and what took place, they were filled with awe, and said, 'Truly this was the Son of God!'
(Matt. 27.45–54)

And when the sabbath was past, Mary Magdalene, and Mary the mother of James, and Salome, bought spices, so that they might go and anoint him.

And very early on the first day of the week they went to the tomb when the sun had risen.

And they were saying to one another, 'Who will roll away the stone for us from the door of the tomb? And looking up, they saw that the stone was rolled back; for it was very large.   And entering the tomb,

they saw a young man sitting on the right side, dressed in

Now after the sabbath, toward the dawn of the first day of the week, Mary Magdalene and the other Mary went to see the sepulchre.

And behold, there was a great earthquake; for an angel of the Lord descended from heaven and came and rolled back the stone, and sat upon it. His appearance was like lightning, and his raiment white as snow. And for fear of him the guards trembled and became like dead men.

a white robe; and they were amazed. And he said to them, 'Do not be amazed; you seek Jesus of Nazareth, who was crucified. He has risen, he is not here; see the place where they laid him. But go, tell his disciples and Peter that he is going before you to Galilee; there you will see him, as he told you.' And they went out and fled from the tomb; for trembling and astonishment had come upon them; and they said nothing to any one, for they were afraid.

(Mark 16.1–8)

But the angel said to the women, 'Do not be afraid; for I know that you seek Jesus who was crucified. He is not here; for he has risen, as he said. Come, see the place where he lay. Then go quickly and tell his disciples that he has risen from the dead, and behold, he is going before you to Galilee; there you will see him. Lo, I have told you.' So they departed quickly from the tomb with fear and great joy, and ran to tell his disciples.

And behold, Jesus met them and said, 'Hail!' And they came up and took hold of his feet and worshiped him.

Then Jesus said to them, 'Do not be afraid; go and tell my brethren to go to Galilee, and there they will see me.'

(Matt. 28.1–10)

We focus on the differences between Mark and Matthew in each of the two cases, for the differences in the telling of the stories reveal the differences between the two 'worlds' of belief and attitude. A casual reading may fail to yield an adequate perception of those differences, but, in the case of the second pair of passages, there is a way of strengthening that perception.

In the Gospel of Peter, the story is repeated in such a way that it may fairly be described as another re-telling of the same story, but in terms so different that this time there is no blinking them. Just as Matthew seems to elaborate and diverge from Mark, so this version (it is the most likely explanation of its origin) moves on

from Matthew, using features from his narrative (and a few
ingredients from John 20–21) but diverging and elaborating much
more strikingly than Matthew did in relation to Mark. But the
principle, concerning the disclosure of 'worlds', is identical in the
two cases.[1]

But the scribes and Pharisees and elders, being assembled together and
hearing that all the people were murmuring and beating their breasts,
saying, 'If at his death these exceeding great signs have come to pass,
behold how righteous he was!' – were afraid and come to Pilate, entreating
him and saying, 'Give us soldiers that we may watch his sepulchre for
three days, lest his disciples come and steal him away and the people
suppose that he is risen from the dead, and do us harm.' And Pilate gave
them Petronius the centurion with soldiers to watch the sepulchre. And
with them there came elders and scribes to the sepulchre. And all who
were there, together with the centurion and the soldiers, rolled thither a
great stone and laid it against the entrance to the sepulchre and put on it
seven seals, pitched a tent and kept watch. Early in the morning, when the
Sabbath dawned, there came a crowd from Jerusalem and the country
round about to see the sepulchre that had been sealed.
   Now in the night in which the Lord's day dawned, when the soldiers,
two by two in every watch, were keeping guard, there rang out a loud voice
in heaven, and they saw the heavens opened and two men come down from
there in a great brightness and drawn nigh to the sepulchre. That stone
which had been laid against the entrance to the sepulchre started of itself
to roll and gave way to the side, and the sepulchre was opened, and both
the young men entered in. When now these soldiers saw this, they
awakened the centurion and the elders – for they also were there to assist at
the watch. And whilst they were relating what they had seen, they saw
again three men come out from the sepulchre, and two of them sustaining
the other, and a cross following them, and the heads of the two reaching to
heaven, but that of him who was led of them by the hand overpassing the
heavens. And they heard a voice out of the heavens crying, 'Thou hast
preached to them that sleep', and from the cross there was heard the
answer, 'Yea.' Those men therefore took counsel with one another to go
and report this to Pilate. And whilst they were still deliberating, the
heavens were again seen to open, and a man descended and entered into
the sepulchre. When those who were of the centurion's company saw this,
they hastened by night to Pilate, abandoning the sepulchre which they

were guarding, and reported everything that they had seen, being full of disquietude and saying, 'In truth he was the Son of God.'

Pilate answered and said, 'I am clean from the blood of the Son of God, upon such a thing have you decided.' Then all came to him, beseeching him and urgently calling upon him to command the centurion and the soldiers to tell no one what they had seen. 'For it is better for us,' they said, 'to make ourselves guilty of the greatest sin before God than to fall into the hands of the people of the Jews and be stoned.' Pilate therefore commanded the centurion and the soldiers to say nothing.

Early in the morning of the Lord's day Mary Magdalene, a woman disciple of the Lord – for fear of the Jews, since (they) were inflamed with wrath, she had not done at the sepulchre of the Lord what women are wont to do for those beloved of them who die – took with her her women friends and came to the sepulchre where he was laid. And they feared lest the Jews should see them, and said, 'Although we could not weep and lament on that day when he was crucified, yet let us now do so at his sepulchre. But who will roll away for us the stone also that is set on the entrance to the sepulchre, that we may go in and sit beside him and do what is due? – For the stone was great, – and we fear lest any one see us. And if we cannot do so, let us at least put down at the entrance what we bring for a memorial of him and let us weep and lament until we have again gone home.' So they went and found the sepulchre opened. And they came near, stooped down and saw there a young man sitting in the midst of the sepulchre, comely and clothed with a brightly shining robe, who said to them, 'Wherefore are ye come? Whom seek ye? Not him that was crucified? He is risen and gone. But if ye believe not, stoop this way and see the place where he lay, for he is not here. For he is risen and is gone thither whence he was sent.' Then the women fled affrighted.

Now it was the last day of unleavened bread and many went away and repaired to their homes, since the feast was at an end. But we, the twelve disciples of the Lord, wept and mourned, and each one, very grieved for what had come to pass, went to his own home. But I, Simon Peter, and my brother Andrew took our nets and went to the sea. And there was with us Levi, the son of Alphaeus, whom the Lord – (had called away from the custom-house).

(Gospel of Peter 8.28–14.60)[2]

That re-telling, whatever its motivations, should leave no room for doubt that in both cases of movement from one Gospel to the

next (Mark to Matthew, Matthew to Peter), strong motives are
present, waiting to be sought and found by study of the details of the
passages themselves, and, where possible, of consistent features of
the Gospels as whole writings. Such an enquiry, if successful, makes
it possible to 'seize' the pattern of the writer's mind in an act of
imaginative grasp and then to return to the individual passages,
seeing their place within the pattern as a whole.

Focussing again on Mark and Matthew alone, what can we 'see'
in the two patterns presented to us, sampled in these passages? As
far as this pair of passages is concerned, it is not difficult to
characterize the general development from Mark to Matthew. It
concerns one of the leading features of contemporary Jewish
religious culture. In writing his version, Matthew has, in relation to
both the death of Jesus and the resurrection, drawn upon the
imagery of apocalyptic literature. The young man, a human figure,
becomes an angel from heaven, the conventional agent of God's
revelations and of his interventions in working out his purpose for
the world.[3] Also conforming to the conventions of apocalyptic
writing, the story now includes amazing and frightening natural
phenomena: the splitting of rocks and the darkening of the sun,
along with the tearing of the curtain in the Temple, and, at the
resurrection, the movement of the stone. Most mysterious (to us)
and staggering of all, not just Jesus' tomb but also those of 'holy
ones' opened and their occupants appeared in Jerusalem after
Jesus' own resurrection. So strong, as we shall see, is Matthew's
impulse as a rule to write 'tidy' stories, without loose ends, that his
failure to answer questions, obvious to us, with regard to this
happening (how long did this go on? what then happened to those
ancient worthies?) must mean that it is for him not an 'event' in a
sequence so much as one item in an apocalyptic 'package'. That
package in itself is, however, well defined. It appears in a form that,
in our terminology, could be described as firmly supernatural and,
in terms of literary category, legendary.

These are not the only instances of Matthew's heightening of the
apocalyptic definition of a passage. In chapter 24, for example,
where he follows closely Mark's own apocalyptic, visionary

material (Mark 13), he took steps to increase the purity of its apocalyptic purpose and to sharpen the definition of its information about the future. Elements of blurring of the supernatural profile, where Mark is concerned, are removed. Thus, Mark 13 contains instructions to followers of Jesus on their behaviour in case of arrest and trial (vv.9–13). They are to be confident and fearless before magistrates, not worrying about the presentation of their case. They will, at the appropriate moment, be inspired with appropriate words. No doubt for Mark such persecution was part and parcel of the coming End of all things which this chapter is (at least in part) concerned to describe.[4] He lived in an atmosphere where such catastrophic fulfilment of God's purpose was on the threshold, indeed coming into being around him. There was therefore, in Mark, a mingling of purely natural events and supernatural phenomena, the former being 'read' in the light of the assured expectation of the latter; and where we might see the one as the attempted explanation of the other, both were seen by Mark as equally 'events', in present and imminent future.

Where Mark mingled, Matthew distinguished. The Marcan passage is transferred bodily to chapter 10 (vv.17–21), Matthew's collection of instructions to Christian missionaries, typified in the narrative by Jesus' twelve disciples. This passage, which gives unequivocally earthly guidance for life in this world, seems to Matthew the fitting location for instruction about the proper demeanour of missionaries who are arrested by authorities. In other words, what Mark saw as a sign of the End, Matthew sees as a fact of everyday life. The effect on Matthew's apocalyptic description in chapter 24, his parallel to Mark 13, is dramatic. With the this-worldly element removed, the whole becomes a much more defined and 'one-tone' apocalyptic package of symbols and portents: supernatural in character, future in reference.

Matthew made a similar adjustment in his treatment of Mark's passage concerning the rewards which a follower of Jesus may properly expect. In Mark 10.28–31, the rewards are both present and future, the two probably seen as almost fused (as in chapter 13). There is the supportive Christian community (the houses and relations the disciple receives, v.30) – yet, a note of realism, 'with persecutions', as in Mark 13 – replacing the natural family[5] forsaken for Jesus' and the gospel's sake, and there is also eternal life. Matthew deliberately eliminates the this-worldly aspect (including, here, the persecutions) and fixes the eye solely on future reward in the age to come, now including judicial power on the grand scale (Matt. 19.27–30).

In 24.37–25.46, Matthew has inserted into Mark's account of the impending crisis a series of sayings and, chiefly, parables concerning the future. Arguably (though it is not central to our present purpose, save to emphasize Matthew's sense of responsibility and purpose), he has derived them largely from what he has taken as hints in the last five verses of Mark 13, that is verses 33–37.[6] (Matthew's parallel, almost word for word, following of Mark ceases at 24.36 = Mark 13.32: thereafter it is a matter of extending and elaborating words and passing images in Mark.) The effect of the inflation of scale at this point is once more to place the future, when apocalyptic visions will turn to realities, in a defined enclosure of its own; then rewards and punishments, held off for the moment,[7] will be handed out. If we go from the brief final verses of Mark 13 to the long series of parables in Matthew, we find ourselves moving *from* a setting in which present and future are in a continuum. In the present, the believers are to watch for a future which is near, and the watching seems to be the vigilance of eager hope. We move *to* a setting where that continuum is minimized. From the present, the believers look towards a future which remains distinct and exerts its influence now by way of threat as much as hope. The command to watch now expresses caution and warning, and dire consequences will follow failure to obey.

In all these cases (including the passages with which we began), there is an unmistakable tendency in Matthew to sharpen the edges of material found in Mark, to increase the definition (of one period in relation to another, for example), and to make plain to the reader the frame of reference within which he is to place himself. There is a removing of uncertainty.

Another feature of Matthew chimes in with the tendencies we have been identifying. He is concerned to settle matters left in the air by Mark. It is as if Matthew, as he read Mark, was continually faced (internally or externally) by a pert, inquisitive child who must have every gap in the story closed. So, for example, it may not be fanciful to see Matthew 1–2, concerning Jesus' origins, as answering a question raised by the tantalizing and abrupt appearances in Mark of Jesus' family (3.21,31–35; 6.1–6). Do these rather dismissive references not leave one asking: who then were Jesus' parents and where exactly was his place of origin (Nazareth, as 1.9 implies, or Bethlehem, as 'son of David' might imply, 10.47f., in the light of Micah's prophecy, 5.2, given that Jesus as messiah surely came of David's line and place)? And does the dismissive tone of Mark's references to Jesus' family, all the stronger and more mysterious if the Mary referred to in 15.40,47 and 16.1 is rightly taken to be his mother (6.3),[8] truly depict their role in his life and work, or should they be given more significance? Can Jesus' family really have been so negative towards him and he towards them, being 'alone', as his followers must be (10.29)? Matthew answers these questions fully, decisively, and in their proper place, at the beginning of his narrative, in chapters 1 and 2. He answers them not out of church archives, for there was no such resource open to him, but, largely, out of prophecy which had been clearly and satisfactorily fulfilled. God had from of old in scripture settled beyond a doubt the matters Mark had left so hazy and so disturbing.[9]

Concern for question-answering exacts its price: the displacement from its commanding position at 'the beginning of the Gospel' of Mark's striking proclamation of Jesus' appearance on the human scene (Mark 1.1–15; cf. Matt. 3.1ff.). All the same, Matthew should be given his due. There is a case for saying that sheer impressiveness is less durable than explanation – so long as the mode of explanation convinces, as, surely, Matthew's convinced those who shared his education and assumptions.

Similarly, the treatment of John the Baptist in Mark leaves room for improvement in the eyes of anyone interested in watertight argument. Did John think of himself as fulfilling the crucial role of

forerunner of the Lord's great day, the returned Elijah prophesied
in Malachi (3.1; 4.5f.)? According to Mark, *almost* certainly, he did.
There are hints and allusions enough to put one on the track:
Malachi is quoted in Mark 1.2; John is probably depicted in the
clothing of Elijah, 1.6; and there is a kind of identification in 9.12f.
– yet one which could profit from 'firming up'. Matthew does not
let the opportunity pass, adding in plain words: 'Then the disciples
understood that he was speaking to them of John the Baptist'
(17.13). Thus it becomes a part of the instruction which Jesus gave
and his followers received and grasped.

In our own present passage, it may be that the matter of the holy
ones who rose from their tombs on the cue given by Jesus'
resurrection owes its presence, at least in part, to this inquisitive
child element. It makes the beginning of an answer (later to be
much developed) to a question about the implications of Jesus'
saving work for those servants of God in old Israel who antedated
his appearance.[10]

We shall consider later, in another context,[11] a further episode
which may be viewed in this light: that of the guard at the tomb,
which Matthew explicitly relates to the Jewish story that the
disciples had stolen Jesus' corpse (27.64). Finally, we can see how
pervasive this tendency was in Matthew's work if we reflect that
the impressive and triumphant ending of his Gospel (28.16–20)
may not improperly be seen as a response to a question stridently
provoked by Mark's ending (16.8). The demand to tell 'what
happened next' was irresistible.

We turn now to another aspect of the contrast between Mark
and Matthew in our passages, perhaps the most immediately
striking of all. They should be read once more, side by side: now, at
the most basic level, has not Matthew *impressed* you more than
Mark? Put his account into visual terms, and is it not spectacular?
A reader who is susceptible to this imagery is virtually compelled,
if not into faith, then certainly into awe-struck attention. The
susceptibility is of course not something to be relied upon now, for
this is an idiom of a long-distant time and place, but an act of
imagination may enable us to feel its power. Clearly, Matthew is

leaving nothing to chance. We have no pretext for reading, then passing lightly on to some other occupation. We have to recognize that in this man's dying and rising, something stupendous is taking place, comparable only to the divine consummation of the course of the world's history, and indeed a foretaste of it. That is what Matthew's signals say.

But let us consider each Gospel in turn, Mark first. It is necessary to read the Marcan passages, excluding from our minds Matthew's parallels, and for that matter those in the other Gospels too – those works, we suppose, have not yet been written. What is the import of Mark's telling of this tale? Is it not to impress upon us the sheer stark horror of Jesus' death, a 'natural' event at one level, full of great squalour and cruelty, but at another level inviting those who have read Mark so far to perceive mysterious divine significance? The horror finds its climax in the shock of that abandonment by God (15.34) which, whether as a matter of the exegesis of Mark or as an idea in theology, defies conclusive elucidation.[12] We feel also the passivity of Jesus, conveyed by his ever deepening fall into silence and, strikingly, by the frequent use earlier in the narrative of the verb 'hand over' (also rendered, where appropriate, 'betray'):[13] he is the one who acts here by being acted upon – the victim of blind human wickedness as also the instrument of God's saving purpose. This purpose is signified in the splitting of the veil of the Temple and in the confession of faith which Jesus' death evokes from the centurion (15.38f.). Both, in the flow of Mark's Gospel as a whole, echo features of its opening statement,[14] which lays out a theological programme. In 1.9–11, heaven itself is split open (the word is identical with that in 15.38) and the voice of God affirms Jesus in his role, addressing him as the beloved Son on whom God's favour rests. So Mark's story as a whole is enclosed, as it were in brackets, constituted by the opening of the way from heaven to earth (with the barriers of 'heaven' and the veil torn aside) and the proclamation of Jesus' true identity.

In these events as depicted, there is an almost stifling sense of control. At Jesus' death, the horror of crucifixion apart, there is nothing remarkable to see, nothing that does not belong to such

examples of depravity in any age or place, nothing to *compel* faith
such as the centurion expresses. Faith which is nevertheless
elicited in such circumstances has about it a special directness and
simplicity. It is both a freely made response and a gift, coming, it
must seem, as from outside the scene itself. It is as pure a depiction
of faith as could be made, and of Christian faith in particular: it is
in the depth of Jesus' suffering that God is recognized freshly and
unexpectedly – by an outsider who comes in a single move to the
heart of God's work. An event on the surface wholly unpropitious
for religious response produces such response at its purest and
deepest.[15]

Mark's resurrection story has a similar character. Quite as
much as the dying words of Jesus, it baffles exegesis at almost every
level. Is this brief passage really Mark's intended ending to his
book or was more planned and never written, or else written and
then lost? Is it meant to reflect credit on the women as the first
recipients of the message or discredit for their fear and silence? But
were they in fact, in Mark's view, silent or merely dumbfounded –
for, if silent, how did Mark suppose the news ever got out? So was
their fear contemptible and culpable (like that of male disciples in
earlier episodes in Mark, 9.6 and 14.50, so that all discipleship is
seen as fraught with risk of weakness and failure) or praiseworthy,
the awe of those who know themselves in the presence of God? And
does the formal contradiction between v.7 and v.8, the command
to speak and the report of silence, represent untidy editing or some
deliberate (if cryptic) meaning? Is there also cryptic purpose in the
presence of the young man, perhaps linked in Marcan intention
with the figure in the garden, 14.51f.?[16] And if cryptic purpose,
what are we to think of the distance of this whole episode (again in
Mark's intention) from history? Further, is there here true hope of
a successful future, signified in a rehabilitation of Peter and his
fellow-disciples, albeit minimally signalled, or is there, more
soberly, just a promise of life with Jesus in 'Galilee'? And finally,
what then is that Galilee – the location, perhaps literally, of Mark's
church, or the lasting testimony to a stage or facet of earliest
Christian life (distinct from those Jerusalem beginnings described

in Acts), or more symbolically the Gentile world (cf. 14.28; Isa. 9.1), the scene for Mark of the church's mission, adumbrated by the Gentile centurion, the first to be converted by the saving death of Jesus?

To none of these questions is it possible to give a final answer, and there is something salutary in simply feeling their cumulative enigmatic force. The reason for this uncertainty in interpretation is partly that it remains unclear how sophisticated in his conceptuality Mark the author was: how far was he a mere reporter and collector of traditions and how far one who set his stories within a framework of beliefs, pictorially and literarily expressed? The lack of clarity is in turn to be laid at the door of Mark's undoubtedly inexplicit manner. He failed to give pointers capable of directing us to a plain understanding of the manner and level of his discourse.

Therefore the interpreter, who is unwilling to shut his eyes to the range of possibilities, finds himself drawn to follow complementary lines of understanding, and, I have already suggested, need not find them incompatible, not just as abstract possibilities but as true respresentations of the author's mind. That is, there was, surely, a conditioning of Mark's outlook by his circumstances, the bread-and-butter aspects of his life, the pressures to which his Christian group was subject; and there was too a shape to his understanding of his Christian allegiance, and in particular of Jesus, which led him to tell his story in the way he did – not just making him include *this* episode and exclude *that*, but leading him to pattern the whole in a certain way and then each and every line within that whole.

In such a context, the difficulty, the subtlety and the richness of the business of confronting these Marcan passages comes home, and their multiple impact upon us finds a justification. A mixed or half-bewildered response to Mark's resurrection story has its own propriety: it is in this story's nature to leave us unsure whether our legitimate response is to be fear and silence or faith and confidence. Who is to say that either of these is to be dispensed with, either to be held exclusively, in the encounter with the divine? Is not Mark a prime witness to the truth that both are wholly and necessarily legitimate? Even in the face of the resurrection message, strangeness fills our minds, and there is no easy, superficial joy, no mere erasing of the horror just contemplated in the story of the cross, two days and a few verses before. Jesus, risen, remains 'beyond', awesome, elusive; just as in his life and death. Such is the effect of Mark. It is aptly captured by Edwin Muir:[17]

> I was a stranger, could not read these people
> Or this outlandish deity. Did a God
> Indeed in dying cross my life that day
> By chance, he on his road and I on mine?

Then Matthew. To attend now to his adaptation of Mark's narrative may be to experience a partly regrettable yet partly welcome sense of relief. The desire for his own version of that relief was perhaps an important aspect of his motives for undertaking his task at all. To a certain kind of spirit, nothing is more unsatisfactory than the ambiguity and profound mysteriousness of Mark, leaving the reader, even surely his first immediate circle of readers who, we may suppose, knew and shared his mind, struck by the complexity and unfathomability of these events. So Matthew was dissatisfied. He was one for whom loose ends were better tied, mysteries better elucidated, and souls better fortified by clear instruction which would bring them into line.

So (to use a personally felt musical reaction to the two narratives) Mark's string orchestra with flutes is reinforced by ample brass and percussion. The whole apparatus of apocalyptic is (admittedly in token strength) brought on to the stage, and even the insensitive reader is left in no doubt that great events are here in train. Most obviously, they are now public, to be seen with the naked eye not intuitively and inwardly perceived. Those present are fully aware of the portents that accompany Jesus' death, and it is those portents, and not an interior grasping of the meaning of Jesus' dying, that elicit the response of the centurion and (here, not in Mark) his companions. It is then an experience not to contemplate but to go away and discuss with one's friends. This, we may feel, is a faith gained by assault (Matt. 27. 51–54.).

Similarly, at the tomb, the soldiers are eye-witnesses. They have no alternative but to react to such an astonishing happening. On the other side, the women too are lucid and confident: fear remains, but great joy accompanies it and confirms its character as awe not fright; and the awkward reference to their silence has been dropped (28.1–10).

We note that this is not the first time that Matthew has opted for the public stage. He did it in relation to Jesus' birth, in the shape of the visit of the Magi (2.1–12) with Herod and his court in the background; and, adapting Mark, he did it at Jesus' baptism by means of the small but significant alteration of the statement from heaven: from words of commission to Jesus alone ('thou art', Mark 1.11), Matthew moved to words of general declaration ('this is', 3.17). Matthew's kind of faith has nothing to be reticent about, no need to pause in wonderment. It is the response of straightforward people to authoritative statement. Matthew's finale confirms all this magnificently, obliterating our memory of Mark's strange ending (28.16–20).

The issues raised by this transference of meaning are of the utmost significance for religion at any time. In sum, the question is that of the relation of faith to assurance. In Matthew's setting, apocalyptic data were a kind of knowledge, or, as we should say, the result (quickly futile, for the expectations came to no reality) of a desperate will to *know*. In this aspect of it, it was a knowing, not for intellectual satisfaction but for the sake of security of soul. It was a desire to know, in circumstances where the alternative might be religious despair, the deepest and most powerful truths of all, relating to God's purpose and goal for the universe. To be within such a circle of knowledge is to receive already a welcome assurance. Matthew chose to side with that aspiration: at all costs (including that of adapting Mark's story) to resolve undesirable tensions with clear knowledge of how things would turn out, and indeed of how they had already turned out in the case of Jesus. God's authentication of Jesus, says Matthew in effect, has been made so abundantly plain, by portents and angelic deeds at tombs, that no one who is not corrupted (by self-interest like the chief priests or bribes like the soldiers, 28.11–15) should resist the claims of Christian faith: belief is no option, it is, morally and by its evidences, obligatory. So, buttressed within their own assurance, the faithful look out on unbelief.

There is here, compared with Mark, a loss of purity, but a gain in sheer power. Which way, we must ask, is closer to the heart of the relationship between ourselves and God? As we read, merely read and consider, we shall surely incline to vote for Mark – and I cannot deny that my account has made it difficult to do otherwise! But there should be pause. It is one thing to vote for Mark in peace and solitude, another to sustain loyalty to his way. There is a question whether a gift that can be refused and that demands a full 'self' to grasp it in all its subtlety and difficulty, is something we have energy to deal with.

In more traditional terms, grace has the character of conquering us – it does not enter into negotiations. If it does not overwhelm, then it loses its character as sheer gift, the very thing that makes it 'grace of God'. Yet there must be a self to conquer, one rich in content, able to do more than acknowledge defeat by the bludgeoning of even heavenly force (the guards 'became like dead men', Matt. 28.4), able rather to savour the gift and be suspended in a moment of choice. Sheer power, even allegedly divine power, corrupts. And if those who are the recipients of the exercise of power are to escape the corruption of their own free hearts, then sheer strength and impressiveness are to be eschewed. What cannot be gained by sheer vulnerable generosity, understated and open, is not worth gaining at all.

Of course Matthew, with his earthquakes and his angels descending from heaven, is a somewhat coarse protagonist of sheer and overwhelming grace, working on the senses first rather than on the heart. Yet if he is a crude symbol of the principle, he reveals its difficulties. We may then better appreciate the delicacy of the interaction by which faith is born. Mark's unwillingness to insist tells us of a more godly kind of power.

The pursuit of an approach to faith in which sheer impressiveness of divine activity receives high profile has side-effects in other areas of reflection, for example in relation to the nature of authority in religion and to the morality of power.

It is notable that Matthew takes many opportunities of affirming Jesus' ultimate if not present power – a power seen in terms parallel, for all their heavenly context, to plain, naked earthly power. Sometimes Matthew achieves this by adapting Mark, sometimes in passages of his own.

There is in Mark much emphasis on the humility and powerlessness of Jesus. Though he performs acts of power by virtue of his God-given authority (1.11,22; 2.10), he came not to be served but to serve (10.45). There is no doubt of the genuineness of his suffering as retailed without masking in the passion narrative. He is abandoned by his followers (14.50) and by God himself (15.34), as he was earlier by family (3.21) and the friends of his upbringing (6.1–6). He does not know when the End will occur (13.32). All the same, as we have already noted, there is ambiguity in Mark in relation to this theme: Jesus is not simply powerless and he has authority from God. Yet Mark seems to link Jesus' authority most specifically with his being 'son of man' (2.10,28), a term whose subsequent use in this Gospel indicates that this authority is intimately involved with his suffering, and necessarily so: 'the son of man must suffer' (8.31); involved also and equally with his vindication (8.38; 13.26; 14.62). That is, 'son of man' seems to represent for Mark that appellation for Jesus which states the vital paradox: that Jesus' destiny is precisely to *be* the one whose destiny it is, endued with God's authority, to suffer and so to be affirmed by him. Nothing is said which so stresses Jesus' triumph as to negate or offer compensation for his humility and suffering; nothing which helps the reader to put it behind him or isolate it as a preliminary and temporary stage in Jesus' career. Rather, the two aspects are fused and we receive no encouragement to separate them out. As we shall see in each part of this exercise, this coheres very well with Mark's mind in every aspect.

For Matthew it is not so. Humble and lowly Jesus is indeed on earth – and Matthew gives it special emphasis in his use of the word *praüs* ('meek', 5.5; 11.29; 21.5). By a subtle allusion, he even reverses a brash and authoritarian feature of David's kingship in describing the gentle and compassionate nature of that of Jesus (cf. II Sam. 5.8 and Matt. 21.14). This gentle aspect of Jesus' activity is emphasized in Matthew's quoting of two passages from Isaiah (Matt. 8.17; 12.18–21). But majesty waits in the wings and is undoubtedly Jesus' most impressive characteristic. The final episode of the Gospel, unparalleled in Mark, establishes Jesus' relationship to the world in terms of authority for ever (28.18), as his relationship with his followers is one of closest intimacy (28.20).

So, humble though he is, even on earth his lowliness must not be seen as weakness, and some loopholes in Mark, leaving room for such a view of Jesus, are closed. It was not that Jesus *could* do no acts of power in Nazareth (6.5), but simply that he *did* not (13.58). His 'goodness' alongside that of God should not be doubted: he spoke only of 'the good' abstractly, not of his own relationship to it (Mark 10.17f.; Matt. 19.16f.).[18] Also, his own centrality in the future triumph of God's purposes is brought out much more than in Mark. It is *his* kingdom which will appear as at any rate a first stage of the events of the End (compare Mark 9.1 with Matt. 16.28; and see also Matt. 13.41; 25.31ff.). So Matthew sharpens and concentrates Jesus' role in relation to 'the kingdom', in a way already found in Paul (I Cor. 15.22–28), for whom Jesus' reign was, it appears, a stage on the way to God's final rule. Luke (22.29f.) and John (18.36) share this picture ('my kingdom') of the future programme. But Mark does not, and in working from his Marcan basis, Matthew uses this idea to strengthen the personal majesty and triumphant role of Jesus quite beyond its place in Mark.

Authority, then, acquires in Matthew new and uncomplicated kudos. Jesus stamps it with his approval, and his followers will also share it at the End (19.28), as they will already in the life of the church before the consummation occurs (16.18f.; 18.18–20). It takes little imagination to see Matthew as attending, in his inclusion of this theme, to church needs which Mark either neglected or ignored. Where Mark only suppresses attempts to establish power as a feature of the disciples' future (10.35–45), Matthew, as in other areas, faces practical problems (here, that of power within the Christian community) with practical solutions; and gives to those solutions cosmic backing (16.19; 18.18). Further, those who receive authority from Jesus must not confine it to the church as a limited community, but enlist all nations in its sphere (28.19) wherein Jesus' teaching rules supreme (28.20).

We cannot tell why Mark was able to leave these matters so much in the air, and, as far as disciples go, to show them as people who are positively denied authority. It may be that he made a deliberate renunciation, Gandhi-like: that is how Jesus was, and that is how his followers should be. Or else that the imminence of the End made such matters superfluous for him. Or, profoundly, that life in relation to God as Jesus makes him known entails the movement of attention away from all such considerations as those which arise insistently in regard to authority as the world sees it. Perhaps Mark should be read as (in our terms) 'spirituality': the Christian must bear suffering (8.34), embrace humility, not seek power. In that case, Matthew has shifted the material into a new key, that of institutional practicalities and even ecclesiastical politics. Whether we praise or blame him for that will depend on our own sense of priorities, even on our mood. Certainly, Matthew's adaptation of Mark has major repercussions. Mark, we saw, fuses Jesus' suffering with his divine vindication: neither must give way to the other and no separation must occur, above all not in the direction of underplaying the suffering and relegating it to the realm of the tragic but merely preparatory. By his portrayal of plain triumph following on, Matthew first among the evangelists reduced the cross to a new status: that of one event in a drama in which more was to happen – and so an event able to be left behind, able to be, if only so slightly, relegated. With such a tendency, Mark would not collude, as indeed Paul before him (I Cor. 1.23). For Mark, the cross is for ever central to that which Jesus showed of God.

It is then a question of styles of authority. Mark exhibits a picture of divine authority in Jesus which is without fear and without anxiety for the consequences of its passivity. It is also easily open to the charge of naivety, especially when it comes to practical life. Matthew guards against that charge but ventures nothing: authority is *in the end* pure power, as those who fail at the test will certainly discover (22.11–14; 25.41–46). Such a prospect might *impress* one towards faith, but will it ever confer the gift?

4

From Resignation to Requital

In the course of this exercise, we have certainly kept in our sights the historical nature of the writings before us: not in the sense that we have engaged in a detailed investigation of the precise nature and course of the events to which they testify, but in the sense that we have had in mind their pastness. It is possible to read of past events and be scarcely aware of that quality. A date in, perhaps, the twelfth century is attached to them; but, as we read, both their distance from us and their precise location in the flow of time is not prominent in our minds. In former times, such reading was normal, now it is less common; but, while it may now be disclaimed in theory and on challenge, it may still take place, whether naively or with sophisticated doctrine about the constant immediacy of written texts (seen as independent of their origins and of that which they describe) to authenticate it. But here, we have sought to maintain that sense of the pastness of Jesus' death, if only as a brake on certain kinds of distortion and fantasy. It happened at a remote distance from us, in a world whose culture we can understand only with difficulty, and the Gospels which tell of it also come from such a world. It is an enquiry into which we have to enter with constant care.

At the same time, we have sought to bring out the realism of focussing on the texts before us. Removed from the events they describe by a process of tradition and a span of years (albeit not much more than forty or fifty years), and themselves also springing from a remote and alien past, the texts are nevertheless in an important sense immediately accessible to us – on the page in black and white. It is as stories, narratives with a shape and an intention, open to us to try to share, that we encounter them. In this exercise we try to hold together these two perspectives.

We may express the second aspect, their narrative character, in another way, one which introduces the personal factor more prominently into the picture. The telling of the story, for example by Mark, is not simply an external act – a putting down on paper, *over there*, a mere depositing of matter. It is an act of a person expressing his 'world'. It is then properly seen as the fruit of an interaction between the story of Jesus himself, first as it actually happened and then as it had hitherto been told, and the 'story' of Mark, that whole process of education and formation which had gone to constitute his being. Whatever the degree of neutrality or self-effacingness a writer brings to his task, the very process of constructing a story, with boundaries and framework, entails a display of total self-expression. The new narration done by Matthew subsequently is the result of a further stage of interaction of stories, Matthew's 'story' (or 'world') coming into play with that amalgam already formed by the work of Mark. What is more, each subsequent reading, if it involves an attempt to enter into the story, entails yet another such interaction. Each reading, each exegesis, means a new amalgam of 'stories' or 'worlds'. In that sense, there is an existential element in every interpretation and every reading, and the more powerful in its demands, whether in terms of belief or of behaviour, the text in question is, the more significant the interaction is likely to be and the more the fact of it demands recognition. In the case of this new part of our exercise, this is undoubtedly the case.

Matthew's version of the narrative of Jesus' passion and resurrection differs from Mark's not only by way of long shared passages, which may be differently worded in significant ways, like those considered in the last chapter, but also by way of a few episodes which are peculiar to his Gospel. Taking the usual view of the relation between the two books, these are additions by Matthew to Mark.

One of the most striking of these additions is the account of Judas' suicide in 27.3–10:

When Judas, his betrayer, saw that he was condemned, he repented and brought back the thirty pieces of silver to the chief priests and the elders, saying, 'I have sinned in betraying innocent blood.' They said, 'What is that to us? See to it yourself.' And throwing down the pieces of silver in the temple, he departed; and he went and hanged himself. But the chief priests, taking the pieces of silver, said, 'It is not lawful to put them into the treasury, since they are blood money.' So they took counsel, and bought with them the potter's field, to bury strangers in. Therefore that field has been called the Field of Blood to this day. Then was fulfilled what had been spoken by the prophet Jeremiah, saying, 'And they took the thirty pieces of silver, the price of him on whom a price had been set by some of the sons of Israel, and they gave them for the potter's field, as the Lord directed me.'

In part, this passage may be seen as an example of a feature of Matthew's mind already explored – the wish to answer questions, to fill gaps in knowledge, and to leave as little as possible of the canvas empty of definite content. Where Mark was content with loose ends, Matthew was not. In this case, the question was: what then happened to Judas the traitor? So the 'woe' of 26.24 must be substantiated.

Matthew was not alone in the early church in finding that Judas' terrible act of betrayal raised issues demanding comment. Luke also found it problematic, both in itself and in its aftermath, but for different reasons than Matthew. One of his motives was in fact, as we shall see, quite contrary to Matthew's attitude to the matter. For Luke was the inaugurator of what was eventually to become a substantial tradition which sought to exonerate Judas or at any rate to open the possibility of his redemption.

Interest in the question of what happened to Judas was partly a matter of curiosity and partly one of justice. Luke dealt with it in both aspects. As far as justice was concerned, Luke was unwilling to admit that Judas was truly responsible for his action. On the contrary, he was suborned by Satan (22.3) and did not act of his own accord: the point is a plain amendment to the opening of Mark

14 which Luke, like Matthew, had as his basic source. There was therefore no question of guilt.

The Gospel of John shared this opinion (13.2), though from a different point of view. In the context of that Gospel as a whole, though the devil is only once besides referred to (12.31), the factor probably uppermost in the introduction of this theme was the desire to see Jesus' mission in cosmic terms; so that his death was no mere human act, just as his life was lived in the presence of 'the world' (viewed comprehensively and in conceptual form) which he had come to save (e.g. 3.16f.). It took more than human agents to bring about this death, which Jesus entered deliberately (10.18, 'of my own accord') and which was in any case the occasion of the devil's being 'cast out' (12.31), the grand exorcism. John's treatment of Judas was, then, far from being (for example) the result of pity or universalist views of the modern liberal brand.

Luke's motives operated on a lesser scale. Judas was exonerated, it seems, as part of a wider indulgence towards all concerned. Even the Jews acted in ignorance and could be forgiven, as Luke repeatedly states, while at the same time their rejection of Jesus had, objectively, brought about their tragic downfall in the war of AD 66–73 (see first Luke 23.34; Acts 3.17; 7.60; 13.27; and then Luke 19.41–44; Acts 28.25–28). And certainly the role of the Twelve in Jesus' death, so disturbing in Mark, is perceptibly lightened (Mark 14.50 is dropped; Satan is the real instigator of Peter's cowardly lapse, 22.31–34; and stress or sorrow makes the disciples' sleep in the garden understandable, 22.45). So Judas profits from his position as one of the group: as if the question were, what then happened to Judas, *one of the Twelve*? Mark's account (14.10) had already drawn attention to this fact about him, and Luke repeated it (22.3). This was after all what made his behaviour so shocking, the fact which cried out for an explanation. So Luke provides an explanation, attributing Peter's denial and the wholesale failure of the disciples at the arrest of Jesus to human weakness – rather than the feeble callousness suggested, to our deep discomfort, by Mark. Judas then failed, but yet *he* did not, and we may pity him alongside those others whose future, as leaders of the young church, was rosier than his.

Judas' membership of the Twelve is then also a factor in Luke's other reference to him, this time in connection with his death. His recounting of this episode (Acts 1.18–20) is in effect a by-product of his telling how the college of the Twelve was re-established by the recruitment of Matthias to fill the vacant place. As to Judas' end itself, creating the vacancy, Luke describes it as a grim accident rather than any kind of punishment.

Luke is, in other words, taking a first step on the way to that vision of Judas' redemption, aligning even him as one with all of humankind in failure and in need, which Edwin Muir set out so movingly as he described his vision of the restoration of all things:[1]

> And Judas damned take his long journey backward
> From darkness into light and be a child
> Beside his mother's knee, and the betrayal
> Be quite undone and never more be done.

For such a vision, Mark had, in fact, in his own dark manner, prepared the ground. For him too there is nothing unique about Judas. True, he, 'one of the twelve', handed Jesus over (14.10f., 17–21, 43f.); but it is crucial to an understanding of Mark's story of the passion to see the common sinfulness, and so the uniform need of redemption, of all concerned in these events (including, of course, the readers). Jesus is in effect rejected and opposed by all – Pilate, priests, scribes, and his own followers. Among the latter, there is no grading here, and certainly no exoneration: Peter who denies (14.29–31, 66–72), the whole group who flee (14.50), and Judas who betrays are of a single hue. 'All have sinned and fall short of the glory of God' (Rom. 3.23) is a kind of rubric standing over Mark's recounting of the passion. In that sense, Judas is at one with everyman, whose desperate need meets the sovereign remedy of Jesus' ransoming act (Mark 10.45), and Mark says no clear word to exclude Judas from the new dawn (16.7), though there is a hint of it in the 'woe' of 14.21 and in Judas' absence at 14.28. All of us are Judas, and for all of us there is the strong/

precarious door of hope. Putting Mark and Luke side by side, we may consider that though exoneration and pity can reflect well on a person's generosity, there is more realism and greater religious depth in the recognition of the seriousness of the human need for a way through – with a death as our route to life.

All this Matthew has crucially amended, and his story of Judas' suicide is the chief sign of his quite different approach. First, like Luke, he individualizes Judas – no longer a symbol of everyman, he is a man with a fate of his own and distinguishable from *us*; but unlike Luke, he shows him no mercy and feels no hint of pathos concerning him. He records Jesus' command to love one's enemies (5.44), but shows little imagination and depth of soul when his story gives him opportunities to live by it. That is true with regard to Judas, as also to the scribes and Pharisees in chapter 23, and even sometimes to 'publicans and sinners' as a lumped-together category of rejects, as in 5.46f. and 18.17. Matthew is not able in this way to sustain the best he knows; just as his expansive sense of the open invitation of the Gospel is quickly qualified by threats of terror for those not meeting some unspecified conditions (22.1–10, then 11–14). Similarly, presumably because of practical difficulties, he cannot sustain Mark's 'pure' doctrine on marriage, spoiling and confusing the vision it embodies by his exception clause (Mark 10.2–12; Matt. 5.32; 19.9): a case where the attempt to be helpful exacts its price.

In the case of Judas, other considerations, especially the belief that justice must be done, come to the fore. So for Matthew, Judas is a man of unutterable wickedness who necessarily gets his deserts. The story is told by a writer of straightforward moral sensibility who has felt the presence of a moral lacuna in Mark's story. To make his point more sharply, Matthew has even intensified Judas' wickedness, in a manner that in the circumstances might be thought pettifogging: according to Mark, Judas was offered money by the authorities (14.11), but in Matthew he asks for it (26.15). Thus he shows a love of riches which is the very antithesis of the love of God and his kingdom (19.22; 22.37). And, here singled out at the supper, he as good as lies outright about the planned betrayal – flagrantly, as the solemn meal begins (26.25). Judas 'out-hypocrites' any scribe or Pharisee (23.13 etc.).

It is true that just as Peter is depicted by Matthew as showing realization of the horror of his denial (26.75), so Judas is said to repent (27.3): Matthew's tidiness of mind demands a reaction from these leading actors in the story to the deeds they have perpetrated. But in the case of Judas, it is not the repentance that may lead one into the arms of a loving and forgiving God but sterile remorse, which drives him speedily to despair and suicide.[2]

That suicide is the just outcome of the story, as far as Judas' part in it is concerned. In numerous passages, Matthew has already shown his concern with requital, whether in the short term or the long. The insertion into Mark (in a passage where he closely follows him) of Matt. 16.27 states the principle and demonstrates his attachment to it. It is replicated time and again: in the parable of the tares (13.40–43), the wedding (22.11–14), the two debtors (18.34f.), the wedding maidens (25.10–13), the talents (25.28–30), the sheep and the goats (25.41–46).[3] Even Pilate's hand-washing (27.24) may be, in part, seen by Matthew as a valid renouncing of responsibility, authenticated by a dream (cf. the role of heaven-sent dreams in chapters 1–2); for the Jews are, in Matthew's view, solely guilty of Jesus' death. They, all of them[4] (27.25; 21.43), were to meet the requital of their deed in the destruction of the Temple in AD 70, to which Matthew looked back with satisfaction as an act of judgment (22.7; 24.15). Moreover, the act of justice which in Judas' case was self-inflicted was assuredly intended by God, for it was foretold in prophecies of Jeremiah and Zechariah, and so inevitable (27.9f.; cf. Zech. 11.12f.; Jer. 18.1–3; 32.6–15).

Some of these elements are not original to Matthew. In Mark already the factual responsibility of the Jews for the rejection and execution of Jesus is seen as greater than that of Pilate (3.6; 14.1, 10f.; 15.14), though he in his weakness (15.15) partakes fully of man's hopelessly flawed condition. But there is a new degree of particularity and of vindictiveness in Matthew. A comparison of Mark 12.1–12 with its parallel, Matthew 21.33–46, shows this up. In Mark there is a hint of sadness, a perception of tragedy, in the

Jews' rejection of the Messiah, which is missing in Matthew: cf. Mark 12.9–11 and Matthew 21.41–43. Here as elsewhere, Matthew ensures the directing of rewards and punishments into the appropriate quarters. Pilate's washing of his hands plays a part in this, and even his wife, a pagan, sees more truth than the Jews – Jesus, she knows, with a perception akin to that of the pagan Magi of chapter 2, is a 'righteous man' (27.19). For Matthew, it is necessary that people should plainly receive their due, sooner or later, if the moral order of the universe is to be safeguarded.

In the light of these Matthean developments, we can see that Mark's story resolutely avoids sidelines. It does not divert from the central thrust of its convictions, in order to deal with marginal matters such as the fate of Judas, and brushes aside the insistent questions (internal or external) to which Matthew responds. Mark does little to gratify concern for mere information – or for mere vengeance. The one may seem frivolous, the other the sign of a superficial morality. Mark, then, tells the story of Jesus' death *straight* – frankly and without mitigation of its central point. The reader is bidden to take all or leave all, when confronted with the demand: how do you react to this picture of Jesus' total impotence before man (14.50) and God (15.34), a picture not even yielding the gratification of seeing the wicked receive their due? Once more, we recall the prominence of the verb 'hand over', the chief verbal instrument of the impression given by Mark that passivity, instanced in Jesus, the one from God, is the necessary and sufficient condition of religious authority.

The addition of the passage about Judas' death brings to light a far-reaching contrast between Matthew and Mark. It is distinct from that discussed in the last chapter but not out of keeping with it. Both contrasts show a certain crude clarity in Matthew, a practical attitude to theology and ethics, twin aspects of the religious outlook. Mark is harder to characterize than Matthew, perhaps because of an apparent reticence (as it seems to us); but he strikes us as disposed to recognize the awesome profundity of the story he must tell and the inadequacy of any treatment which would trivialize it in the least degree.

The contrast between the two evangelists, discerned by way of the Judas passage, leads on to further reflections. Implicitly, it raises a question which we can envisage in a first-century setting and then move through to our own time and place: if you follow Jesus, are you permitted to interest yourself in requital, insist on people receiving fair treatment, or must you brush such a principle aside under the pressure of a quite different sense of God's dealings?

We have already seen that Matthew is inclined to betray a duality of outlook – to announce generous moral principles which he then seems unable to sustain. The love of enemies does not extend in practice to scribes and Pharisees, who surely represent for Matthew the most significant enemies he faced, Jews of his day who were interested enough to oppose his doctrine. They gave him his most testing opportunity to display that love. The command to refrain from judging, again, does not prevent him from expressing censorious opinions about those whom he rejects or from whom he differs, including Judas (7.1–5; 18.5f., 15–20). Formally, it may be, he sees himself in these cases as reporting God's condemnation, with Jesus as its mouthpiece, something distinct from personal judging of one's fellows. All the same, the invoking of divine support for objects of disapproval and the envisaging of an appalling end for them is a game that all can play. In terms of practical moral policies, Matthew's bias is for requital, despite his more constructive impulses.

In Mark, it is as if the summons of Jesus in the light of the nearness of God's kingdom is so urgent that there is no time to pause for such discriminatory exercises. It is not so much that the principles involved are denied as that they are pushed to the margins of concern. Forgiveness of others is enjoined, 'so that your Father also who is in heaven may forgive you your trespasses' (11.25); but the principle is not rammed home as in Matthew, where it is repeatedly stated (6.14f.; 18.21–35) and where the threatening negative implication is made explicit: 'So also my

heavenly Father will do to every one of you, if you do not forgive
your brother from your heart' (18.35).

There are other, less direct symptoms of the same contrast. In
Mark 9.40,[5] there is a statement of the principle that, in relating to
inadequately authenticated supporters, disciples of Jesus are to be
welcoming and positive, giving them the benefit of the doubt. The
boundaries of the church are not to be high or rigid: 'he that is not
against us is for us'. In the light of Mark's Gospel as a whole, we
should suppose that the overwhelming urgency of Jesus' summons
gives absolute priority to the need to respond to his call: that alone
really counts, and the niceties of precise relationship with the
Christian group are secondary. In the crisis, all are welcome to
support Jesus' cause, and the well-disposed are not to be turned
away. As always in Mark, what matters is to 'follow', in the true
and not the superficial sense perceived by the disciples (9.38).

In the context, Matthew omits the relevant passage, but he has a
similar saying in another setting, 12.30, only the sense is reversed:
'he that is not with us is against us'. Here, the question of the
boundaries of the Christian community is able to be viewed in its
own right. There is now time for sober consideration of questions
such as this. So rapidly, the human tendency to define the outsider
has stepped to the fore. In that perspective, the opposite conclusion to Mark's imposes itself. Not 'all welcome', but 'you're in or
you're out'. Christians need to know where the boundary fences
are located. It is no accident that Matthew alone of the evangelists
has a sufficiently formal sense of the church as to lead him to use
the term in his narrative, at the price, surely, of anachronism in
relation to Jesus' lifetime (16.18; 18.17).

If we turn to the question of attitude to groups who might be
seen as peculiarly exposed to adverse judgment, there is the same
dual position: contrast between Matthew and Mark, *and* ambiguity in Matthew himself occasioned by generosity not sustained.
Matthew is expansively open-armed to the Gentile mission in the
solemn and impressive conclusion to his Gospel (28.19). But he
can still use 'Gentile' as a term of perhaps unthinking abuse
(18.17). And where Mark sees the incident in the Temple as

symbolizing the extension of the scope of God's holiness and salvation to 'all nations' (Mark 11.17), Matthew, in dropping the phrase, shows that he sees it as the enforcing of due reverence in the house of God (Matt. 21.12). Similarly, while tax collectors are accepted into the company of Jesus in Matthew as in Mark (Mark 2.13–17; Matt. 9.10–13), the former can still refer to them as, with Gentiles, in the category of the outcast. It is as if Matthew tolerates the principle of free and unconditioned acceptance as the basis for relationship with Jesus, but cannot wholly face its implications. The point is striking: it has come to our notice a number of times, from different vantage-points. It amounts to this: in the tension between mercy and justice, Matthew cannot see God's love as having, ultimately, free rein. So, above all in his appalling espousal of eternal punishment, he blunts the gospel he seeks to proclaim, to the point of removing its wonder as gospel.[6]

We return to the question: can Christian ethics function in practice on a policy of non-retribution, and simply by presenting us with Jesus who conveys God's free acceptance of us? (Take care of the theology and the ethics will look after themselves!) In terms of human need, there is a choice of policies: do we require, for the health of our relationship with God, instructions which we may then obey (such as Matthew – it is no accident – provides in abundance)? Or else, the gift of a status of intimacy with him, one whose responsibilities and opportunities we may then learn to embrace? In this matter, there is no utterly clear-cut division between our two evangelists, for Matthew includes as attractive a statement of the priority of Jesus' call to a new standing in relation to God as can be found anywhere in early Christian writing: 'Come to me, all who labour and are heavy laden, and I will give you rest. Take my yoke upon you, and learn from me; for I am gentle and lowly in heart, and you will find rest for your souls. For my yoke is easy, and my burden is light' (11.28–30). In effect, Matthew may be seen – and practical people will applaud him – as doing justice to both policies. But, for all his clarity of statement and all his practicality, is such a doing of justice satisfactory? It means combining warm invitation with dire threat of rejection in case of

failure to achieve the required standard. Such a combination runs
the risk of failing both religiously and ethically. It extinguishes
both the freedom of the one who wishes to give himself to God and
the genuinely moral quality of the promised relationship. It
involves an ethic of overhanging sanctions and not of restoration or
re-making. Matthew's high sense of utter goodness as our duty is
vitiated by his coercive tendencies; and, again, the very character
of the gospel is endangered.

Mark, on the face of it less realistic, achieves greater consistency.
It is likely and understandable that Matthew's shift from Mark in
the directions we have identified is linked to a less urgent sense of
the nearness of the End and consequently a greater need to provide
guidance for life's difficulties and problems. But, if this is correct,
Mark's eschatology has the beneficial effect of purifying his
objectives: the call and the gift of God are all. His purpose for
mankind is redemption, restoration. Mark sets before us his sense
of this restoration, conveyed through his chosen medium, the story
of Jesus, at two levels.

In the story as a whole, the dominant strand is the intercourse of
Jesus with certain groups – disciples, scribes, Pharisees, his family.
The leading impression of these relationships is dark and full of
foreboding: there is, it seems, to the very end, no guarantee of good
emerging. Human redemption, we must feel, is a matter of the
utmost difficulty and achievable only by way of the most profound
crisis. Only Jesus' death can win us any benefit, and our fate hangs
by a thread.

But this precarious aspect of the gospel of salvation does not
stand alone. In the encounters of Jesus with individuals, we have
so many vignettes of salvation achieved. By meeting with Jesus,
each is brought to 'live', to 'see', to 'follow', to be 'forgiven', to 'give
all' (5.41; 8.25; 10.46–52; 2.5; 12.41–44). In Mark, these encounters taken together have a position of great prominence in
the narrative, a position obscured in Matthew who, while
reproducing many of them, includes so much teaching material
that their impact is reduced. For Mark they represent acts by
which salvation, total well-being before God, is generated. They

are exemplars of that which is available equally for Mark's readers. Again the question comes: is such a simple gospel sufficient for human need or is it unrealistic in the face of man's profound incapacity to live rightly? Can there then be a satisfactory provision of moral guidance which does not in effect sap the relational structure of our dealings with God or bring with it the whole corrupting apparatus of promises and threats, rewards and punishments? Such an apparatus sets ethics on independent feet, apart and adrift from its subordination, in a Christian context, to the gospel.

In Mark (and predominantly in Christian practice for the greater part of the church's history), the reader is hard put to it to distinguish between what we now describe as doctrine, spirituality, ethics and pastoral theology, seen as separate spheres of interest and enquiry. To set them apart in the context of this Gospel is to falsify. The unified nature of Mark's concern is itself salutary for us, who are accustomed to compartmentalizing our theological studies. But in Matthew, there are (it is another way of expressing the point already made) signs of a severance of one line of interest from another, setting one somewhat at variance with another – doctrine (belief in Jesus and his saving mission from God) vying with ethics (the demands of requiting justice), ethics somewhat at odds with pastoral need. The question arises whether Matthew's move, however strongly and inevitably it was pressed upon him in the circumstances of his time and place, is not a symptom of lamentable developments, as yet unforeseen.[7]

The reader may feel that in this chapter especially there has not been entire success in avoiding anachronism, identified as a bogey early in the book. For, has not Matthew been subjected to a peculiarly modern liberal scrutiny and been denied that right to 'be himself' which was put forward as a necessity for any valid 'listening' to him? The danger dogs the interpreter at every turn, catching him sometimes when he feels most safe. But there has been care in this discussion to keep attention on some of the more constant factors affecting man's relationship with God, however varied the patterns in which they present themselves in different historical contexts. All the same, it is undeniable that when we make our act of sympathy with Matthew, our (let us say) liberal sentiments quickly colour our discernment. What for Matthew may well have seemed a satisfactory collocation of themes seems to us full of tensions. But we cannot be sure. It may be that, as he confronted Mark and took the step of altering him, Matthew himself was pulled to the limits, forced into adjustments to circumstance that he would have preferred to have avoided, and well aware that in his making provision for practical Christian living in an imperfect church he had put the very meaning of Jesus at risk. The more we swing once more away from the text to a sense of his circumstances (and some of his difficulties are not altogether unlike ours), the more we may feel that, for all his inner conflicts, Matthew's synthesis is by no means lacking in grandeur.

5

From Intimation to Demonstration

In the interests of another line of enquiry, we return to a passage discussed in chapter 3.

> And when the sabbath was past, Mary Magdalene, and Mary the mother of James, and Salome, bought spices, so that they might go and anoint him. And very early on the first day of the week they went to the tomb when the sun had risen. And they were saying to one another, 'Who will roll away the stone for us from the door of the tomb?' And looking up, they saw that the stone was rolled back; for it was very large. And entering the tomb they saw a young man sitting on the right side, dressed in a white robe; and they were amazed. And he said to them, 'Do not be amazed; you seek Jesus of Nazareth, who was crucified. He has risen, he is not here; see the place where they laid him. But go, tell his disciples and Peter that he is going before you into Galilee; there you will see him, as he told you.' And they went out and fled from the tomb; for trembling and astonishment had come over them; and they said nothing to any one, for they were afraid.
>
> (Mark 16.1–8)

Now, suppose that this brief narrative were all that had been written or that had survived concerning the resurrection of Jesus. We then notice the following features. We should possess no record of resurrection appearances by Jesus, only the promise of appearances to come ('there you will see him', v.7). As we saw in chapter 3, there is ambiguity about any action taken by the women: did they speak as instructed; or did they really remain silent, for if they did, how did the message ever come to be known? We are struck by the absence of any credentials for the young man: who is he that anyone should heed his words? True, for the reader of Mark, he merely confirms what Jesus had prophesied (8.31; 9.31; 10.34; 14.28), so that the news does not come unexpectedly. All the same, he is a mysterious figure who, in the imagined sequence of events if not in the Gospel as a whole, is given no accreditation. Moreover, the word used for him (*neaniskos*) raises the enigma of his relationship (if any) with the similarly designated figure in 14.51f.[1] There is finally the question of the trustworthiness not only of the young man, but also of the women: what kind of witnesses are these? We may of course believe because we trust Mark or because we are his Christian readers (in the first century or the twentieth), readily walking alongside him; but as followers of the story sequence itself, we are simply *required* to trust, and Mark takes no trouble to give us grounds for doing so.

If then this account were all we had concerning Jesus' resurrection, and supposing that resurrection to be integral to Christian faith (as Mark would surely have us think), we should be compelled to be believers on the basis of sheer trust, as opposed to well-based evidence or alleged knowledge. That is, the style of faith required would be self-abandonment to a mysterious divine initiative with consequences yet to be seen, not judgment concerning a set of plain happenings. Further, the act of faith would not be a single act of decision in relation to the evidence, after which 'belief' could be said to *have been* reached; but a continuous process of contemplative engagement with the story and its significance. You would keep asking: what *is* this resurrection? Who exactly is this risen one? Deterred from easy or settled conclusions, you would seek to go on learning – not in regard to factual assurance but at the level of insight and understanding. You would hope to go on finding new levels of religious possibility as you engaged in a movement 'into' God.

Matthew's presentation of the matter is quite different in total effect if not wholly in content. On the common theory of the relation between the two Gospels, he has taken and used Mark, but added to his account – and at first sight his additions look religiously trivial, just added details. But this is no mere incorporation of extra information; it is a transformation of significance. His narrative may be considered in two sections.

1.

Next day, that is, after the day of Preparation, the chief priests and the Pharisees gathered before Pilate and said, 'Sir, we remember how that imposter said, while he was still alive, "After three days I will rise again." Therefore order the sepulchre to be made secure until the third day, lest his disciples go and steal him away, and tell the people, "He has risen from the dead," and the last fraud will be worse than the first.' Pilate said to them, 'You have a guard of soldiers; go, make it as secure as you can.' So they went and made the sepulchre secure by sealing the stone and setting a guard. (Matt. 27.62–66).

While they were going, behold, some of the guard went into the city and told the chief priests all that had taken place. And when they had assembled with the elders and taken counsel, they gave a sum of money to the soldiers and said, 'Tell people, "His disciples came by night and stole him away while we were asleep." And if this comes to the governor's ears, we will satisfy him and keep you out of trouble.' So they took the money and did as they were directed; and this story has been spread among the Jews to this day. (Matt. 28.11–15).

2.

Now after the sabbath, toward the dawn of the first day of the week, Mary Magdalene and the other Mary went to see the sepulchre. And behold there was a great earthquake; for an angel of the Lord descended from heaven and came and rolled back the stone, and sat upon it. His appearance was like lightning, and his raiment white as snow. And for fear of him the guards trembled and became like dead men. But the angel said to the women, 'Do not be afraid; for I know that you seek Jesus who was crucified. He is not here; for he has risen, as he said. Come, see the place where he lay. Then go quickly and tell his disciples that he has risen from the dead, and behold, he is going before you to Galilee; there you will see him. Lo, I have told you.' So they departed quickly from the tomb with fear and great joy, and ran to tell his disciples. And behold, Jesus met them and said, 'Hail!' And they came up and took hold of his feet and worshipped him. Then Jesus said to them, 'Do not be afraid; go and tell my brethren to go to Galilee, and there you will see me.' (Matt. 28.1–10).

Now the eleven disciples went to Galilee, to the mountain to which Jesus had directed them. And when they saw him they worshiped him; but some doubted. And Jesus came and said to them, 'All authority in heaven and on earth has been given to me. Go therefore and make disciples of all nations, baptizing them in the name of the Father and of the Son and of the Holy Spirit, teaching them to observe all that I have commanded you; and lo, I am with you always, to the close of the age.' (Matt. 28.16–20).

What is the effect of this narrative? Is it not to reverse the characteristics we observed in Mark? First, unmistakable appearances of Jesus occur: to the women, in relation to their visit to the tomb, then to the eleven disciples (the male leaders of the church) in a concluding episode of climactic splendour and universal power, looking confidently to the future. Second, the women's action is made clear: they act in obedience to instructions and pass on the message (28.8,10), which is promptly obeyed (28.16). Third, the messenger has clear and reliable credentials, for he is an angel from heaven, no less than God's messenger, seen by the firmly non-Christian soldiers. He reminds us (Matthew is fond of such backing) of the prominent angelic activity at the time of Jesus' birth; so this high authentication frames the story, at its beginning and its ending. In Matthew's view, such reassuring support has been only just off-stage throughout (26.53). And in their own way, the soldiers, muzzled by the bribe of the Jewish authorities, are also good witnesses to the truth of Matthew's story of the Easter morning event (different though it is from that which Mark had told him). Finally, the women are also depicted as good witnesses: they report with confidence. Whereas in Mark there was, in terms of the story, no special reason to trust them, here there is no special reason to doubt them, especially in view of the unimpeachable authority of the angel at the head of the whole story.

In sum: Matthew provides us with a tale to be used with assurance. Here is the material for a catechist's account of Jesus' resurrection. The message now is: believe this, a story that is coherent and strong, with all Mark's gaps carefully filled, and you will be well grounded in faith.

We may compare the two patterns of existence presented by Sir Henry Harcourt-Reilly in Act Two of *The Cocktail Party*:[2] practical, useful routine which keeps life going and yields commendable stability; and then the other way:

> The second is unknown, and so requires faith –
> The kind of faith that issues from despair.
> The destination cannot be described;
> You will know very little until you get there;
> You will journey blind. But the way leads towards possession
> Of what you have sought for in the wrong place.

Matthew shows no great sympathy with such faith. The copper-bottoming of resurrection belief, presented as information which there is no reason to disbelieve, was, in Matthew's view, not his invention. Prophetic scripture is an infallible argument for him: so in 12.40, the story of Jonah provides a compelling parallel and forecast for what has now taken place. Portent too carries great weight: so, as we have seen, at Jesus' death, Matthew has told us of the resurrection of the holy ones, itself foretold in Dan. 12.2 in not dissimilar words, an authenticating escort for God's messiah, such as the legions of angels might also easily have provided (27.52f.; 26.53), and, as announcing his supreme dignity, such as the Magi did provide in Jesus' infancy.

Now, in the resurrection story itself, objections are anticipated and answered. 'It is quite simple, the disciples stole the body from the tomb.' 'But no, that is an inspired and wicked rumour. It happened thus: soldiers were present (not, according to Matthew, strangely, at the resurrection itself – were they, for him, not worthy?) at the angel's rolling away of the stone and the tomb's discovery as empty, and were bribed to hold their tongues.' While Matthew thus answers questions naturally present in the air, there is still a measure of reticence: the soldiers did not witness Jesus' emergence alive from the tomb, as they did in the later Gospel of Peter.[3] Oddly, in Matthew's presentation, Jesus had, it seems, actually left the tomb before the stone was rolled away. As we saw, at this point, the Gospel of Peter satisfied still further the insatiable demand to have all enquiries answered and faith provided with a water-tight case.

We cannot tell how heavy a price it was for Matthew to pay, this positive contradicting of Mark – we have too light a grasp on the psychology which led him to his work; nor do we know how easily he got away with it – we know nothing of the immediate circumstances of his writing or of the first using of the Gospel. Nor, again, is it fruitful to speculate[4] on the source of the episode of the soldiers as recounted in Matthew or the process, of transmission by which it reached the shape we observe in the Gospel of Peter – though the latter, being more of a visibly literary process, at least offers itself to the eye. How much was gossip, how much Matthew's own construction, we cannot tell. Luckily, the question of source is not germane to our purpose. Our interest is in ways of telling the story and in conceptual implications of the alterations which we observe as Mark is superseded by Matthew. To recapitulate: this interest has two aspects, not easily distinguishable in practice: the intentions of the writer and the reactions of the modern reader. There are two questions: 1. what did Mark (then Matthew, then others who retold the story) intend to convey? 2. How does the story, in its successive versions, strike *you*? Though the questions are distinct, they are easily assimilated in the answering, as the reader attributes to Mark or Matthew the meaning which he himself discerns, feeling that the evangelist must have seen as he himself sees. Yet, try as one will to 'listen to' the evangelist in his own right, there must remain a speculative element in any answer to the first question, for direct evidence is unavailable; whereas answers to the second at least have the objectivity and accuracy that accompany self-testimony. Though our interest in this exercise is in both aspects, realism has made us focus initially and with greater assurance on the second, while hoping not to betray too grossly the claims of the first.

The process of adaptation which we have surveyed in these passages is, at the lowest level, a tidying up, and we have already seen enough evidence to show that this is a leading feature of Matthew's work as he handled Mark. It appears in the addition of the episode concerning Judas; it occurs in his explanation (17.13) identifying John the Baptist with the returned Elijah. It also marks a passage like 16.17–19, clarifying Peter's role in a wholly positive way, where Mark left, shocking and unalloyed, the identification of the disciple with Satan (Mark 8.29–33). (Matthew retains the difficult words, but his addition gives them a much more reassuring setting – Luke dealt with the difficulty by omitting them altogether, 9.18–22.) It appears too in other episodes concerning the disciples, such as Mark 8.21 (cf. Matt. 16.12), where their incomprehension of Jesus' words as reported by Mark (Do you not yet understand?) is boldly replaced by its opposite (Then they understood). Here then is Matthew in his now familiar mood, removing obscurities and tying up loose ends. He is, it seems, out to satisfy his readers' minds, in one way or another.

But religiously, the change effected by Matthew is more serious. Focussing now once more on the changes before us in the passion and resurrection narrative, we may say that it testifies to a surrender to the desire for more 'facts' and the achieving of a water-tight case for the beliefs of Christians. Matthew's changes can be best explained by sensing his dissatisfaction with Mark on this score. Mark had left the story vulnerable to uncertainty and to rebuttal. Too many points were left open and unclear, and all kinds of possible explanations might be offered by friend or foe. Matthew shuts the door on such speculations by telling a story which is, as far as possible, impenetrable to invaders. All queries can be swiftly dealt with, all objections quickly ejected.

In one way, the instance now before us is marginal: this brief tale about the bribing of the guards – in how many people's faith, then or since, has it played a role of any importance? Who has seriously said that he would be convinced of Christian claims if only he could be shown that the disciples did not steal Jesus' corpse from the tomb? But in another way, it is not marginal at all. If Jesus' resurrection is central to Christian faith, then having proof of it, stopping up leaky holes in the case for it, may well seem vital. It all depends on how you view Christian faith.

It has to be confessed that 'Christian doctrine' as a pursuit among Christians has rarely been slow to pick up Matthew's hint in more substantial ways: to build up the water-tight case, and to identify and then answer questions on the grand scale. From earliest times, and at many levels of sophistication, it has been among the strongest impulses to theological writing and one of the leading characteristics of controversy. We may think of the work of Justin Martyr in the second century, answering objections to Christianity raised by Jews, Irenaeus and Tertullian a little later, countering Gnostics and others, Athanasius replying to objections from both Jews and Greeks, and then the whole scholastic structure of medieval theology, whose programme and ideal was the building up of a rounded structure of belief, argued out at every stage (to select at random just a few moments in the story).

Such an approach to Christian doctrine has seemed both natural and unassailable. After all, the church has received a revelation and has a gospel to proclaim. Both these modes of seeing faith (in terms of *revelation* and *proclamation*) invite the giving of 'proof', the conveying of conclusive argument and the dismissal of objectors.

In the early years of the church, the process was fortified and then established as virtually unchallengeable by other factors, notably the appeal to Christian origins and to apostolic tradition, from which deviation was disallowed.[5] The working out of this notion was, we now see, full of fantasy and myth-making, but it carried conviction everywhere and enhanced the identifying of faith with certainty. So did the intellectual pattern of the classical period of Christian doctrinal statement, the first five or six centuries of the church's life.[6] That pattern remains influential not only because of its permanent effect on important continuing strands in Christian theology, but also because it is enshrined in the great credal formulas of christendom. As a result of its underlying Greek philosophical assumptions, that classical expression of Christian teaching has a curious two-sidedness, never satisfactorily resolved. On the one hand, it is convinced of the essential ineffability and unknowability of God, man's incapacity to capture the divine in human speech; but on the other hand, its picture of the relation of heaven to earth, with the latter in certain ways the 'shadow' of the former, led to the eternal being of God, in particular his trinitarian nature, being 'read off' from earthly analogies (such as the allegedly tripartite structure of the human personality, for example with its capacity to remember, understand and will).[7] In effect, then, a profession of essential ignorance was balanced, and overshadowed, from this side too, by the claim to knowledge.

From all these diverse impulses, what we referred to as Matthew's 'hint' proved to be but the start of a mighty process, to which the unregenerate human tendency to curtail God to manageable dimensions, thereby the more easily to negate his essential religious claims, added its contribution.

Yet the more this track is followed, the more its falsity becomes apparent, as far as the human response to God and quest for God are concerned. The more the alleged certainty is found, the more holes in argument and evidence are blocked, the more God himself eludes us. Faith is faith is faith. It is 'the conviction of things not seen' (Heb. 11.1). 'We walk by faith, not by sight' (II Cor. 5.7). 'Blessed are those who have not seen and yet believe' (John 20.29). Three distinct New Testament writers establish the principle – the last of them in connection with the resurrection, to which Matthew reacted so differently. The principle enforces, and embraces, the plain truth that 'revelation' is always channelled by way of limited and conditioned human minds – though that is, no doubt, a way of putting the matter which is more convincing now than in earlier days.[8] Pointing in the same direction is the haunting example of Jesus, whose 'proclamation' was parabolic in character, and on that very account open-ended, leaving much to the hearer.

It is Mark who insists most firmly (supporting his insistence by the contents of his Gospel) that Jesus taught exclusively in parables (Mark 4.33f.). In terms of our present exercise, and in line with this fact, the lesson is: be content with Mark's story, with its tentativeness and openness; do not strain to fill gaps, thus ignoring the ethos of faith which Mark so carefully creates. Follow Mark, and you have the chance of receiving the mysterious love of God which can never let us rest with any assured and permanent picture of life or belief. Mark communicates, above all in his final chapters, a faith, centring on Jesus, which comes by intimation not demonstration. While that style of faith has of course never ceased, there is virtue in raising the question of its compatibility with its rival, with which it has so often muddled along in uneasy tandem.

What emerges from the comparison of texts in this chapter is thus a deep contrast between two major approaches to religion. We have moved from an attempt to 'hear' the New Testament writers to questions of attitude to 'doctrine' as a phenomenon in Christian life (and it is in many ways, because of our history, a peculiarly Christian phenomenon, with only imperfect analogies in other religions). From a consideration of attitude, we have moved to a sense of the risks run by weak humans with tidy minds and timid souls who do not much relish being people of faith, in the Marcan sense.

It is of course preposterous to suggest that Mark and Matthew set forth convictions on these great matters, foresaw their significance, or formed clear conclusions about them. What we 'hear' as we attempt to listen to them, not interposing our own speech, is necessarily conditioned by centuries of Christian thought and activity and by our present setting. We listen with ears attuned in particular ways, including a sensitivity to the dichotomy of attitude we are now considering. All the same, while two great roads may pass through the land far from each other and be fully visible to all, they may start close together at some obscure junction and as only barely discernible tracks. It is not unjust to see them as already having the promise of the major routes they eventually become. So, implicit in Mark and Matthew already there are differences of outlook which were to be crucial in their effects, and in their Gospels we witness Christians already reacting to pressures inevitably felt by religious people in ways that found permanent counterparts in Christian life.

We can go further, now turning to the evangelists once more with a historical eye. For all we know, what we discern as characteristics of Mark, including those features brought out in this chapter, he was aware of in only limited ways. They were indeed his, but they were not held with full deliberation. But in the case of Matthew using him, it cannot have been quite the same. There must have been, for the critique of Mark and the consequent adaptations to be made at all, a high degree of self-consciousness. In whatever spirit it was spoken, the word was: 'I shall write not *this*, but *that*'; and the changes came from willed decisions concerning not just innocuous matters of style and vocabulary, but significant and even crucial issues of belief. When a writer acts thus, he cannot help but disclose the whole 'world' in which his being moves: his fears and perplexities and preferences, the goals he will do much to achieve, and the tendencies of mind he regards as erroneous or dangerous. And, even across great chasms of cultural difference of all kinds, we can express sentiments of agreement or rejection; and in so far as being in the same Christian tradition has any reality, then we simply must. For though Christianity has been a constantly changing and shifting thing, often deluding itself about unaltering faith and institutions, yet there are also continuities and at the very least there is the willing recognition of common allegiance, a shared commitment gladly made.

6

Villains and Realists

In each of the comparisons made between Mark's and Matthew's telling of the story of Jesus' death and resurrection, and in the resulting reflections, Matthew has come off badly. His very clarity has shown him up all the more. Others making the same comparisons will undoubtedly arrive at quite different evaluations. This does not necessarily mean that they have committed the error identified earlier as the interposing of their own voices across those of the evangelists to whom they should have been trying to 'listen'. They may have heard the same messages as I in the two Gospels, but responded in the light of other judgments of value.

I have found myself (there is no denying) awarding prizes to Mark and presenting Matthew as, however understandably, the villain of the piece, inferior and even reprehensible at almost every turn. Time and again, he has seemed to spoil the purity of Mark's teaching as embodied in his story. This has surely raised the question: had not Matthew better be laid aside, and is not his dominating popularity from earliest times deeply regrettable? If he really did so distort the earlier Gospel, expressing such lamentable tendencies of mind and soul, we can surely dispense with his services. We should be grateful only for the fact that these tendencies, easily identifiable by the modern approach we have adopted, were not so visible in former times and were not among the reasons for that popularity. And this is, of course, quite apart from the issue of where the authentic voice of Jesus himself is to be found – an issue with which this exercise is not strictly concerned; though it has done nothing to encourage the view that Matthew was in a position to reach behind Mark, delving into better tradition, in order to reproduce it. All through, our focus has been on the last stage of the process: the import of the story as narrated, revealing the mind that tells it.

But that sour conclusion is not the only possible moral of my tale. For not only have we found Matthew diverting Mark in the use he makes of him into undesirable channels; we have also found that in each case, Matthew's change of direction has been thoroughly absorbed into the continuing flow of the Christian tradition. As a result, no one who shares in that tradition (even only by way of shared 'recognition' of commitment) can remove himself from the effects of Matthew's decisions. Many-shaped and multifarious, they have been too deeply pervasive for any of us, even if willing, to expel them easily. The perception of God's movement towards us (and towards others more particularly) in terms not of 'gift', freely offered and to be freely received, but of 'assault' by spectacular force; the perception of the ultimate morality of the universe in terms not of the power/weakness of a loving, non-resisting God, but of deserts, to be enforced by sanctions; and the perception of faith in terms not of gracious suggestion, to steal upon the believer and pervade his whole being, but of sealed and impregnable demonstration: all these have long become endemic in great tracts of Christian thought and practice. The three perceptions merge into unity on either side, producing two conflicting styles of religion. It is not too much to say that there is much of Matthew in each of us and that complex pressures in society and church impel us to move his way – in effect, to retell the story for ourselves essentially along his lines.

The reaction then must surely be: have we the stomach and the freedom of heart to 'hear' Mark, who first ventured to write the story of Jesus, and performed his task, so it seems, with such amazing spiritual clarity? That would, however, be too sudden and too simple a step. We have no reason for supposing that

Matthew made his changes of direction as some kind of apostasy. He was, as all the evidence of his book shows, wholly devoted to Jesus, whom he saw as God's gracious, saving gift to his people. That gift, identified with the all-embracing kingdom of God, was for Matthew precious beyond price (Matt. 13.44f.). We considered earlier his sublime words of divine welcome to those who know their need of God, given by Jesus whose yoke is easy and burden light (11.28–30). He gave us Jesus' pronouncement of total blessedness before God, in 5.2–12, and the sublime assurance of his presence, in 28.20. He included parables which, if they speak of divine vengeance, also display God's prodigal generosity: the servant forgiven his massive debt (18.23–35), and the outsiders brought into the feast (22.1–14). Matthew is then, from our present point of view (and especially from the side of morality, as we saw in chapter 4), ambiguous. If he does not transcend a picture of a God whose grace and justice are in perpetually unstable equilibrium, the reason is not far to seek, once we turn back from the story itself to its historical setting.

In the course of this exercise, we have repeatedly observed the twofold tendency in modern studies of the Gospels: on the one hand, towards historical reconstruction of the context in which they arose, leading to a grasp of their meaning in that setting; and on the other hand, towards a purely literary appreciation of them as narratives. We have observed too that while the former has the appearance of objectivity and of close relationship to evidence, it is fraught with danger, for the lack of hard facts bearing at all closely on the matter in hand from outside the Gospels themselves. The latter, while offering limited results and inviting us, in the interests of a type of aesthetic attention to the text, to put aside the historical interest which most of us cannot now shed, has at least the merit of realism and strict concern with accessible evidence: it works with what we have, *these* words on *these* pages. We have refused throughout to accept that it is either desirable or necessary to choose between these methods (while fully recognizing their several features), and have sought to maintain a twin perspective on the two Gospels which have been our chief concern. Each tells its story in its own special way, and that story must be seized in its nature as narrative; but each must also be seen in its pastness and as, at least potentially, evidence for the setting in which it arose. There is the chance that it can give us many clues to the perspectives and priorities of the Christians in whose circle its ideas were formed and its composition undertaken.[1] Plainly, the clues are scarcely ever direct, for these are books ostensibly about the lifetime of Jesus, and even when they look direct (as in John 21.24), they are hard to elucidate. So the task is full of difficulty, and those who are suspicious in these matters of even the controlled use of the imagination are likely to steer clear of it.[2]

That leads them to be suspicious of a great deal of modern study of the Gospels, especially the various kinds of redaction criticism of the last twenty-five years. Much of it has centred on the attempt to discern the evangelist's mind on certain major themes: the person of Jesus, the role of his disciples, the Jewish law, the mission of the church, and the coming End. More recently, attention has been directed, perhaps still more precariously, to the social setting of the community behind each Gospel:[3] its attitude to those around, its relation to matters of family, wealth, and poverty. To revert to language used earlier, the Gospel has been 'interrogated' from these points of view (and, some would say, been made to answer, whether or not it had anything to say!). Though there has been much scholarly divergence, it is undeniable that, despite the sceptics, the application of these styles of historical sensibility has been widely appreciated and has produced a degree of consensus on many aspects of the Gospels.

For our present purposes, it is the fact of this kind of enquiry that is chiefly important, rather than the accuracy of particular conclusions to which it leads. So we recognize that neither Mark nor Matthew wrote in a void, where social, economic and church realities are concerned. Their ideas were not 'pure' ideas, but were undoubtedly conditioned by various pressures, difficulties and opportunities. They wrote not for us but for circumstances of immediate particularity.

We have already had occasion to refer to one of the most widely agreed differences between the beliefs of the two evangelists who concern us. For Mark, the sense of the nearness and urgency of the End is in the forefront, though it is less clear whether this is a matter of his holding to the earliest Christian outlook in this respect or reviving it in a crisis in his own day (occasioned perhaps by Nero's persecution in AD 64 or by the Jewish revolt of AD 66–73). In Matthew, the source of fevered urgency has passed and there is a striking sense of a longer perspective, in the light of which Christian life has more of an earthly future ahead of it. The evidence for this conclusion lies in some of the alleged consequences of the shift: notably, the prominence in Matthew, by contrast with Mark, of the full provision of useful teaching for moral and ecclesiastical purposes, and the re-siting of some of the eschatological material in contexts concerned with day to day activity. It is moreover not being over speculative to infer the preoccupations of Matthew from the amount of space he chose to give to certain subjects: the morale and life-style of Christian missionaries, under the guise of the Twelve, are dealt with at length in chapter 10, as is the pastoral discipline of the church in chapter 18. The need to promote harmony and forgiveness recurs time and again in relation to both personal and communal life (5.21–48; 6.12–14; 7.1–5; 18.21–35; 20.25–28). It is evident from these and other symptoms that Matthew felt the pressure of long-term practical needs to a much greater degree than Mark. He was therefore all the more exposed to forces pushing him towards the perceptions which we identified in the narrative of Jesus' death and resurrection. In Matthew's circumstances of thought and culture, such forces as these had the effects that we discerned. With us, no doubt, they would be different but analogous.

Mark's sense of the imminence of the kingdom of God in its fullness was, by contrast, the necessary condition of his purity. Because of it, he could keep himself 'unspotted from the world' and preserve before God a directness that suffered no competing distractions. There was simply no need to make provision for questions arising in relation to so many aspects of life: family, property, disputes and structures of authority. In all these matters, a brisk message of renunciation is adequate. It is a matter of single-minded response to the summons of God.

Yet, in terms of these expectations, Matthew deserves praise for his realism. The basis of Mark's purity of faith, so far as it depended on prophecy of the End, literally perceived, was falsified by the failure of his kind of hope as it slipped into new forms in the face of non-realization;[4] and it is hard to see how his vision of things could be translated into public policy. In that sense, Matthew deserves, in principle, not only our understanding but our commendation.

But he cannot simply be accepted on his own terms. It is possible to envisage responses to the changed situation which avoided some of the pitfalls into which he stumbled. The changes of perception which we have observed were not inevitable and change could go in other directions. The Gospels of Luke and John show precisely how that was so. Many have found their alternative solutions, in relation both to the big issues and to the smaller but congruous matter of the telling of the story of Jesus' death and resurrection, much more attractive and much less disturbing.[5] Their solutions, moreover, are more visible to the naked eye. Their differences from Mark's passion and resurrection stories are much more striking. Because his alterations to Mark have seemed so few and so marginal, Matthew has generally been discounted when it has come to the narrative of the passion. For that reason alone, as well as for the sharp way in which he holds up the mirror to us, it has been worth looking further into his apparently trivial changes and additions to Mark.

All unwittingly, Matthew holds up the mirror – to readers not one whit less ambiguous or flawed than he as he strove to shape his faith to life's demands. For us, in our time and place, the appropriate response will of course be different, but Matthew speaks to us in both the grandeur and the limitation of his vision, inspiring and warning us.

As for Mark, the enigma remains to the end. We have discovered profundity chiefly in his giving of the last word to God's mysterious redemptive call and in his willingness to leave room for the believer's moral and religious freedom. He does not bludgeon us with thunderbolts from heaven, or frighten us into goodness with the prospect of future terrors. Nor yet does he cow us into a kind of believing by piled up arguments and evidences. He seems rather to keep his distance, in a passivity akin to that of Jesus in his suffering. But is this really such a reticence as the refined modern reader of liberal inclinations can respect and value? Or is it a rough unfinishedness, brought about by the overwhelming assurance of the kingdom of God, an assurance of such magnitude that it puts Matthew's paltry backing of his beliefs by little certainties about tombs into the shade? Is then Mark the one whose faith is, in his own eyes, demonstrated up to the hilt, and are we quite wrong to see instead gentle intimation? Here, most crucially, what the text says to us, speaking as sheer text, and what Mark said through the text, speaking as himself, may be most at variance. Nevertheless, as far as this world counts evidence, Mark is content with a sort of agnosticism. His trust in the end, however vivid the imagery in which he might have expressed his faith, was in God alone, of whom Jesus in his weakness/authority had been the emissary. If all our complaint turns out to be that Mark purely *believed*, then we can be glad to stretch out to him after all, for encouragement and for rescue.

There is a final lesson to be drawn from the comparison which has engaged us. From one point of view it may seem that the changes Matthew made to Mark are after all less than fundamental. They are matters of religious attitude rather than belief, and shared belief can express itself in a variety of such attitudes. It may, however, be more salutary to reflect that religious attitudes reflect what people truly believe, how they 'see' God and respond to him, more genuinely, perhaps, than their avowed beliefs. So here, our evangelists face us with two disparate theologies, two conceptions of God, between which, though never lightly, one must choose.

People have always read the Gospels in the hope of taking steps towards God or opening themselves to him. The Gospels are for use as windows giving on to the divine, means to a greater end. The ways in which they serve that end have been many and diverse. Over the greater part of Christian history, they have been taken, in effect, as *sheer words*, as from God, without primary awareness of their original setting. There was little sense of the author as distinct from his book, a person with a life and context apart from his book and expressed within it; or of the narration as distinct from the events described. Modern study of the Gospels has placed wedges at all these points. It has placed the evangelists against their backgrounds and viewed them in their common humanity, focussing on the particular character of each as a person who wrote *thus* in a specific time and place. Such treatment, by contrast with earlier ways of reading the Gospels, undoubtedly 'de-divinizes' both the evangelists and their books. But it does nothing to hinder us from entering into the pictures of God and the implicit beliefs about him to which they testify, and having entered, pondering; and having pondered, deciding what, in the light of other truth we know, we may make our own, often obliquely. These old evangelists do not close discussion or monopolize the formation of modern Christian lives: they contribute towards it and invite our attention as part of a wider process of faith.[6]

Epilogue:
Post-critical spirituality

The foregoing exercise is now complete. That is, as an exercise in listening to the Gospels. In that sense, it has been an exercise within the sphere of New Testament studies. But constantly it has given rise to reflections which go beyond New Testament studies as currently practised. Some of these reflections belong to the spheres of basic doctrinal questions, others relate to more detailed issues in Christian belief, still others to important ethical matters. Some readers, however, may find themselves prompted to even more fundamental considerations – especially about the whole status of critical theology in relation to the heart of the religious disposition, the believer's awareness of God and relationship with him. This epilogue simply offers a meditation on this subject which some who have read so far may, perhaps after a gap, find a useful conclusion.

A Case to Answer

Is praying upset or made more difficult by the critical study of theology? If so, at what level and by what right? We begin with the matter of mood. Like an affectionate friendship, prayer rests on trust and stability. On that basis, it aims to build constantly. It aspires to ever deeper love and commitment. By contrast, the study of theology in a critical spirit is based on loyalty to criteria of truth and evidence derived from outside the theological field altogether. It aspires to detachment and objectivity. Instead of resting on settled decision, it asks for its constant postponement. The two atmospheres could hardly be more different.

But the contrast would only matter if one felt required to approach the same objects in both ways. It might be held that that need not happen. Prayer is directing the attention to God and is quite different from the business of trying to talk sense about him. In prayer, there need be no question of verbal formulation; in theology no question of attending to the Being, the outer areas of whose property one is trying to map.

Yet that frontier, just describable in theory, is in practice tricky to identify, trickier still to maintain. There is so much traffic across it that its very existence is called into question.

In the first place, can wordless, thoughtless attentiveness to God have the field to itself in prayer that is Christian? Christianity says things about God, has ideas about him, chooses between the options which mere theism leaves unsettled (e.g. is God aloof or near, loving or uncaring?). And the praying Christian has no business to exclude his belief about God's character as he turns to him. Indeed the very ground of his turning is that God is precisely loving, generous and dependable.

Moreover, much praying is of a less refined brand and at a less elevated level than this discussion has so far suggested. Or at any rate, it uses tools and aids, most of them verbal and documentary. Above all it uses the Bible. In its traditional expressions in office and eucharist, it uses it extensively and constantly, and meditative prayer is fed from those sources.

Yet once prayer turns to ideas and words, it risks straying across the frontier into theology's land. And if in former days, the two lands lived at peace, two provinces of a single country, responsible for two aspects of a single enterprise, that can no longer be relied upon. Frontier guards may at any moment arrive to challenge the stray to produce credentials. With its loyalty to criteria of truth and evidence derived from outside the traditional religious field, theology asks for reflection and self-conscious questioning about the ideas, words and writings which prayer is content simply to use as aids to self-forgetting love. What is their origin and pedigree? In what historical circumstances did they arise? Of what style and kind were the people who coined them? How do they rate for intellectual coherence? Will they stand up to interrogation?

It is not simply that these questions alter the tone; as if prayer, caught by surprise, could happily retreat again across the frontier unaffected regarding the incident as closed. It is true that prayer may return quite simply enriched: a greater knowledge of background and literary structure may help the prayerful use of the servant chapters of Isaiah or the Psalter.

But prayer may instead return confused and even battered. Confused, for example, by engaging in a proper and thorough exegetical study of the Birth Stories in the Gospel of Luke. Certainly, the tone of the study was different from the tone appropriate to their liturgical or meditative use. But that awkwardness might be easily overcome – one is used to analysing a poem and still being moved by it, and enjoying a Shakespeare play 'done' as a set book.

If confusion may be overcome, battering may take more curing. Supposing prayer set great store by the virginity of Mary, then might the exegetical study, in the name of truth, give a licking to the truth hitherto valued? Supposing prayer set great store by the Risen Christ and study of the origins of the idea left it dim and unsure, might not the licking be intolerable? How many such assaults could prayer survive? Might prayer even die?

An Answer to the Case

A frontier there may be between prayer and theology, but they are certainly provinces of a single divine empire. That is the truth never to be lost sight of. Does that mean restoring the pre-critical situation, when this position was clearer? Of course not. Despite all impulses to fortify the frontier, so that it cannot be crossed (even to build a wall to stop observation), or to reduce theology to vassal-status, hoping to keep it in an archaic condition or insisting that it speak only sweet words, the situation is quite different now. The Enlightenment occurred! Moreover, it occurred (so prayer and theology must agree) within the empire of God. However surprising it may be, the voice that speaks up for the claims of evidence cries on his behalf.

But does not that mean giving theology the whip-hand, giving it the power to dictate to prayer and enslave it? If prayer were to take the full force of critical theology, accommodating doubt where it can legitimately be raised and accepting new patterns of faith which offer themselves, would it not be transformed and probably impoverished out of all recognition?

It may be that the situation is so serious that the possibility of such transformation has to be faced. The important thing is to resist the impoverishment and rather to endow with Christian riches. The frontier is becoming neglected, overgrown, in places barricaded. It is time to open it up to fresh and busy traffic.

Understandably, the apparatus of prayer is the object of tenacious conservatism. Attachment to God easily involves attachment to the symbols and words which aid attention to him. It is true that many Christian churches have recently seen extensive modernizing of liturgy, both text and scenery; but much of the impulse was conservative: whether for the revival of early models, as sought by the liturgists, or for the re-affirmation of deep Christian spiritual principles (e.g. the fellowship of the people of God), which were felt to have been too long obscured.

It is one thing to understand conservatism, another thing to leave it unchallenged. When the critical theologian turns to prayer (feeling both provinces to be open to him for he is God's servant), he may see his primary task as recalling Christians to certain principles of the faith:

1. That idolatry is the constant threat to true religion. Just as in theology it may emerge as insensitivity to the shifting setting of language and ideas, so in prayer it expresses itself in false attachment to practices and beliefs which intellectual integrity excludes.

2. That human words and ideas concerning God are always relative, approximate and inadequate. Theology and prayer both know this perfectly well upon a moment's reflection – but, by long habit, neither is good at acting upon it persistently. The

consequence is that both theology and prayer must be ready to shift their ground, in what may seem at the time to be fundamental ways, if compelled by considerations of truth – and this on the very terms of their belief concerning God's essential transcendence.

3. That critical theology can therefore hold its head erect in the company of prayer. Far from feeling itself to be a threatening and embarrassing neighbour (even a potential traitor), it may recognize its place, in a historical perspective, as the heir, in our post-Enlightenment culture and post-Christendom society, of that traditional emphasis in Christian thought on the negative side of man's approach to God; to which Platonism gave first intellectual clothing but to which the cross of Jesus, as the embodiment of God's being and character, gave prior and definite expression.

Theology (and only with loss of integrity can it now not be 'critical' in style and method) and prayer have a single responsibility to the truth of God, but discharge it differently. Undoubtedly, in our culture, for a variety of reasons, there is an inevitable difference of tone and atmosphere. It is trivial if that alone is felt to be daunting. There is also a hard task of doctrinal reconstruction, accepting new perspectives and patterns. In this task, theology and prayer should join forces, in the persons of those who see the need and are willing to work at it. It may take a deeply contemplated theology of the cross to make the moves required. And prayer itself may nerve theology's arm, purify its spirit, and lead it profitably through its life-giving deaths.[1]

NOTES

Foreword

1. See the following works: C. F. Evans, *Explorations in Theology 2*, SCM Press 1977, Part I; *Resurrection and the New Testament*, SCM Press 1970; J. C. Fenton, *Preaching the Cross*, SPCK 1958; *The Passion According to John*, SPCK 1961; A. M. Ramsey, *The Narratives of the Passion*, Mowbray 1962; W. H. Vanstone, *The Stature of Waiting*, DLT 1982.

1. *Hearing the Gospels*

1. J. L. Houlden, *Connections*, SCM Press 1986.
2. *Connections*, ch. 3.
3. Attempts to stem the tide find no real point of purchase in the actual world of theological teaching and research; see, e.g., Lesslie Newbigin, *The Other Side of 1984*, World Council of Churches, Risk Books 1983; *Foolishness to the Greeks*, SPCK 1986.
4. *Connections*, ch. 2.
5. Including both specialized techniques of interpretation, especially of scripture, such as allegory, and the purely verbal appeal to biblical and other sources, with minimal sense of their historical context. See Robert M. Grant and David Tracy, *A Short History of the Interpretation of the Bible*, SCM Press 1984.
6. There is the paradox that in a secularized ethos, theology has proved so fertile that the number of academic disciplines under its broad umbrella increases constantly, well beyond the traditional biblical, doctrinal, historical and ethical studies; largely by the making of marriages with other disciplines such as psychology, sociology or anthropology.
7. See Bruce Chilton, *Beginning New Testament Study*, SPCK 1986; W. G. Kümmel, *The New Testament: the History of the Investigation of its Problems*, SCM Press 1972.
8. For a discussion of this subject, see Norman R. Petersen, *Rediscovering Paul: Philemon and the Sociology of Paul's Narrative World*, Fortress Press, Philadelphia 1985, especially Introduction; also, in relation to a Gospel, David Rhoads and Donald Michie, *Mark as Story*, Fortress Press 1982.
9. For the journey backwards into the text and forwards again, as a procedure of interpretation, see J. S. Dunne, *The Way of All the Earth*, Sheldon Press 1973; *A Search for God in Time and Memory*, Sheldon Press 1975.

2. *Matthew Among the Gospels*

1. For the early influence of this Gospel, see Edouard Massaux, *Influence de l'Évangile de saint Matthieu sur la Littérature chrétienne avant saint Irénée*, Publications Universitaires de Louvain 1950.

2. On these matters, and on the thought of the Gospel, to which our attention will soon turn, see the following: Donald Senior, *What are they Saying about Matthew?*, Paulist Press/Fowler Wright Books 1983; Paul S. Minear, *Matthew: the Teacher's Gospel*, DLT 1984; Richard A. Edwards, *Matthew's Story of Jesus*, Fortress Press, Philadelphia 1985; Graham Stanton, *The Interpretation of Matthew*, SPCK 1983; G. Bornkamm, G. Barth, and H. J. Held, *Tradition and Interpretation in Matthew*, SCM Press 1963; J. D. Kingsbury, *Matthew as Story*, Fortress Press 1986.

3. For the relationship of the first three Gospels (the Synoptic Gospels), see C. F. D. Moule, *The Birth of the New Testament* (3rd ed.), A. & C. Black 1981, Excursus IV by G. M. Styler; W. R. Farmer, *The Synoptic Problem*, Macmillan 1964.

4. For accounts of the thought conveyed in Mark's narrative, see Ernest Best, *Mark, the Gospel as Story*, T. & T. Clark 1983; Ralph P. Martin, *Mark, Evangelist and Theologian*, Paternoster 1972; Morna D. Hooker, *The Message of Mark*, Epworth 1983; Werner H. Kelber, *Mark's Story of Jesus*, Fortress Press Philadelphia, 1979; William Telford, *The Interpretation of Mark*, SPCK 1985.

5. This perception of the sectional nature of the make-up of the Gospels is the foundation doctrine of form criticism; see W. B. Tatum, *In Quest of Jesus*, SCM Press 1982, ch. 2.

6. This is of course no more than hypothesis, but see Étienne Trocmé, *The Passion as Liturgy*, SCM Press 1983.

7. See, for example, the works listed in the note to the *Foreword* to this book.

8. See especially Ellis Rivkin, *What Crucified Jesus?*, SCM Press 1986; Martin Hengel, *Crucifixion*, SCM Press 1977; Ernst Bammel and C. F. D. Moule (eds), *Jesus and the Politics of his Day*, Cambridge University Press 1984.

9. Most obviously, quotations from and allusions to scripture, seen as fulfilled in the events relating to Jesus. Note, above all, the role of Psalm 22; 41.9; Zech. 13.7, among other passages.

10. Matt. 1.21; 1–2 passim; 11.28–30.

3. *From Gift to Assault*

1. For a much more detailed (and different) account of the story in the Gospel of Peter, see J. D. Crossan, *Four Other Gospels*, Winston Press, Minneapolis 1985. The Gospel of Peter is a work dating from around the middle of the second century and perhaps of Syrian provenance.

2. The Gospel of Peter in E. Hennecke (ed.), *New Testament Apocrypha*, Vol. 1, second impression SCM Press 1973, pp. 185–6.

3. For a discussion of the nature of apocalyptic, see C. Rowland, *The Open Heaven*, SPCK 1982; John Bowker, *The Religious Imagination and the Sense of God*, Clarendon Press 1978.

4. 'In part' because much in Mark 13 seems intended to find a first fulfilment in the story of the passion itself which immediately follows. There numerous details, such as the notes of time and the importance of 'watching' (vv. 35f.), are picked up, as if to say that Jesus' death itself has the climactic and determinative quality in man's relationship with God which is associated with the notion of 'the End' (see

R. H. Lightfoot, *The Gospel Message of St Mark*, Clarendon 1950, ch. IV).

5. It is interesting that the one relation not forsaken by the budding disciple is the wife; and we may read 10.2–12 alongside this passage. Mark sees the decision to follow Jesus almost, but not quite, in individual terms, and shows himself an early Christian advocate of the nuclear family!

6. See M. D. Goulder, *Midrash and Lection in Matthew*, SPCK 1974, ch. 20.

7. Cf. this point also at 13.30 and, less explicitly, 13.49.

8. See J. C. Fenton, 'The Mother of Jesus in Mark's Gospel and its Revisions', in *Theology* LXXXVI, 1983, pp. 433ff.

9. On Matt. 1–2, see R. E. Brown, *The Birth of the Messiah*, Geoffrey Chapman 1977.

10. The belief that Jesus' death was 'valid' for the salvation of pre-Christian people was encapsulated by the fourth century in the credal doctrine of the descent of Christ into Hades.

11. See below Chapter 5.

12. Jesus' words quote Ps. 22.1, and that psalm gives a context of reflection (on the suffering and then ultimate confidence in vindication of a servant of God) in which we may read Mark. But in no way does that reflection 'settle' the meaning of Mark's story.

13. The significance of *paradidōmi* is discussed in W. H. Vanstone's *The Stature of Waiting*, DLT 1982.

14. On Mark 1.1–15, see Morna D. Hooker, *The Message of Mark*, Epworth 1983, pp. 7–16; John Drury, 'Mark 1.1–15: An Interpretation', in A. E. Harvey (ed.), *Alternative Approaches to New Testament Study*, SPCK 1985.

15. Many of Mark's stories have this character, with someone coming upon the scene, drawn by Jesus, and risking 'all' in devotion to him: the woman with the haemorrhage, 5.25–34; the blind man, 10.46–52; the woman who anointed, 14.3–9; and, without contact with Jesus, the widow in the Temple, 12.41–44.

16. Both passages use the same word, and there are other links, suggesting for him some symbolic role (e.g. as the aspiring follower of Jesus, linked to him in death and resurrection): see Frank Kermode, *The Genesis of Secrecy*, Harvard University Press 1979, ch. III.

17. From 'The Killing', see Edwin Muir, *Collected Poems*, Faber, and Oxford University Press, New York 1960, p. 225.

18. Matthew probably did not, however, amend Mark 13.32, despite some manuscript evidence to the contrary.

4. From Resignation to Requital

1. See 'The Transfiguration', *Collected Poems*, Faber, and Oxford University Press, New York 1960, pp. 198ff.

2. The grim story of Ahithophel, II Sam. 17.23, is often seen as having helped to form Matthew's depiction of Judas' end.

3. Matthew is by far the most explicit New Testament source for the later powerful doctrine of God's eternal punishment of the wicked, especially in 25.46. Apart from the single instance in Luke 13.28, he has a monopoly of attributing to Jesus the prophecy which 'sews up' the future occupation of the damned: 'there shall be weeping and gnashing of teeth'.

4. Matt. 27.25 is the leading New Testament authority for anti-semitism among Christians. Of course Matthew envisaged no such future for his words, and we must

see them in a context of what was still in part one of intra-Jewish conflict (or just emerging from such a context). Nevertheless, the words show the same absolute spirit in Matthew which we have already observed.

5. On this example, see further J. L. Houlden, 'The Development of Meaning', in *Theology* LXXXII, 1979.

6. We may compare the wrestling with this issue by one such as Julian of Norwich, with her deeply moral and brave avowal that 'there is no wrath in God'. See Robert Llewelyn, *With Pity, Not With Blame*, DLT 1982; and *Julian: Woman of our Day*, DLT 1985.

7. See G. Theissen, *Biblical Faith: an Evolutionary Approach*, SCM Press 1984, p. 168, considering the crucial moral case for Matthew's integrity, that of love for enemies (cf. p. 46): 'Jesus' love of his enemies seems to have been an impracticable dream in world history so far. But the time could come – indeed is already here – when our survival depends on how far we are successful in reducing aggression between human beings and changing our ways of reacting to enemies.' 'His mode of existence could offer a chance of survival.'

5. *From Intimation to Demonstration*

1. See p. 81, n.16.
2. T. S. Eliot, *The Cocktail Party*, Faber, and Harcourt Brace Jovanovich 1950.
3. But see p. 24.
4. *Pace* J. D. Crossan, see p. 80.
5. See Robert L. Wilken, *The Myth of Christian Beginnings*, SCM Press 1979.
6. See M. F. Wiles, *The Making of Christian Doctrine*, Cambridge University Press 1967; *The Remaking of Christian Doctrine*, SCM Press 1974.
7. See J. N. D. Kelly, *Early Christian Doctrines*, A. & C. Black 1958, p. 276.
8. Especially in view of the modern sense of cultural relativism; see D. E. Nineham, *The Use and Abuse of the Bible*, Macmillan 1976.

6. *Villains and Realists*

1. As H. C. Kee has, for example, attempted to show in the case of Mark: *Community of the New Age*, SCM Press 1977.
2. See John Muddiman, 'Like an Owl in the Desert . . .', *Theology* LXXXIX, 1986, pp. 349ff.
3. See n. 1, above; also R. E. Brown, *The Community of the Beloved Disciple*, Geoffrey Chapman 1979.
4. New forms: whether a sense that the life of the world to come was in effect already enjoyed within the confines of the Christian community (as the Gospel of John seems to hold); or the effective postponement of the End to an indefinite future (as the Gospel of Luke holds, at least in some degree).
5. See n. 4 above, and the books referred to above in *Foreword*, n. 1.
6. Anyone wishing to proceed to a detailed study of Matthew's narrative of the passion of Jesus should read D. P. Senior, *The Passion Narrative According to Matthew*, Bibliotheca Ephemeridum Theologicarum Lovaniensium 39, Leuven 1975; N. A. Dahl, *Die Passionsgeschichte bei Matthäus*, New Testament Studies 2, 1955–56, pp. 17–32. And for Mark, see W. H. Kelber (ed.), *The Passion in Mark: Studies in Mark 14–16*, Fortress Press 1974.

Elilogue: Post-critical Spirituality

1. A version of this epilogue appeared in *Spirituality in Ordination Training*, ACCM Occasional Papers 9, 1980.

INDEX OF BIBLICAL REFERENCES

II Sam.

5.8 — 38
17.23 — 81

Ps.

22 — 80, 81
41.9 — 80

Isa.

9.1 — 33

Jer.

18.1–3 — 47
32.6–15 — 47

Dan.

12.2 — 59

Micah

5.2 — 29

Zech.

11.12f. — 47
13.7 — 80

Mal.

3.1 — 30
4.5f. — 30

Matt.

1–2 — 29, 47
1.21 — 80
2 — 48

2.1–12 — 35
3.1ff. — 29
3.17 — 35
5.2–12 — 68
5.5 — 37
5.21–48 — 70
5.32 — 46
5.44 — 46
5.46f. — 46
6.12–14 — 70
6.14f. — 49
7.1–5 — 49, 70
8.17 — 38
9.10–13 — 51
10 — 70
11.28–30 — 51, 68, 80
11.29 — 37
12.18–21 — 38
12.30 — 50
12.40 — 59
13.30 — 81
13.40–43 — 47
13.41 — 38
13.44f. — 68
13.49 — 81
13.58 — 38
16.12 — 61
16.17–19 — 61
16.18f. — 38, 50
16.19 — 39
16.27 — 47
16.28 — 38
17.13 — 30, 61

18 — 70
18.5f. — 49
18.15–20 — 49
18.17 — 46, 50
18.18–20 — 38
18.18 — 39
18.21–35 — 49, 68, 70
18.34f. — 47, 50
19.9 — 46
19.16f. — 38
19.22 — 46
19.27–30 — 28
19.28 — 38
20.25–28 — 70
21.5 — 37
21.12 — 51
21.14 — 38
21.33–46 — 47
21.41–43 — 48
21.43 — 47
22.1–10 — 46, 68
22.7 — 47
22.11–14 — 40, 46, 47
22.37 — 46
23 — 46
23.13 — 47
24 — 26, 27
24.15 — 47
24.17–21 — 27
24.36 — 28
24.37–25.46 — 28
25.31ff. — 38, 47
25.41–46 — 40

Matt. (Cont.)		8.25	52	15.34	31, 37, 48
25.46	81	8.29–33	61	15.38f.	31
26.15	46	8.31	37, 56	15.40	29
26.24	43	8.34	39	15.47	29
26.25	47	8.38	37	16.1–8	22f., 55
26.53	58, 59	9.1	38	16.1	29
26.75	47	9.6	32	16.7	32, 45, 55
27.3–10	43	9.31	56	16.8	30, 32
27.3	47	9.38	50		
27.9f.	47	9.40	50	*Luke*	
27.19	48	10.2–12	46, 81	9.18–22	61
27.24	47	10.17f.	38	19.41–44	44
27.25	47, 81	10.28–31	27	22.3	43, 44
27.45–54	21f.	10.29	29	22.29f.	38
27.51–54	34	10.30	27	22.31–34	44
27.52f.	59	10.34	56	22.45	44
27.62–66	57	10.35–45	39	23.34	44
27.64	30	10.45	45		
28.1–10	22f., 35, 57f.	10.46–52	52, 81	*John*	
28.4	36	10.47f.	29	3.16f.	44
28.11–15	36, 57	11.17	51	10.18	44
28.16–20	30, 35, 58	11.25	49	12.31	44
28.16	58	12.1–12	47	13.2	44
28.18	38	12.9–11	48	15.15	11
28.19	39, 50	12.41–44	52, 81	18.36	38
28.20	38, 39, 68	13	27, 80	20–21	24
		13.9–13	27	20.29	63
Mark		13.26	37		
1.1–15	29	13.32	28, 37, 81	*Acts*	
1.2	30	13.33–37	28	1.18–20	45
1.6	30	13.35f.	80	3.17	44
1.9–11	31	14.1	47	7.60	44
1.11	35, 37	14.3–9	81	13.27	44
1.22	37	14.10	44, 45, 47	28.25–28	44
2.5	52	14.11	46		
2.10	37	14.17–21	45	*Rom.*	
2.13–17	51	14.21	45	3.23	45
2.28	37	14.28	33, 45, 56		
3.6	47	14.29–31	45	*I Cor.*	
3.21	29, 37	14.43f.	45	1.23	39
3.31–35	29	14.50	32, 37, 44, 45, 48	15.22–28	38
4.33f.	63	14.51f.	32, 56		
5.25–34	81	14.62	37	*II Cor.*	
5.41	52	14.66–72	45	5.7	63
6.1–6	29, 37	15.14	47		
6.3	29	15.15	47	*Heb.*	
6.5	38	15.33–39	21f.	11.1	63
8.21	61